The Golden Legend

Henry Wadsworth Longfellow

Contents

PROLOGUE. 7
THE SPIRE OF STRASBURG CATHEDRAL. 7
I. THE CASTLE OF VAUTSBERG ON THE RHINE. 10
II. A FARM IN THE ODENWALD 27
III. A STREET IN STRASBURG. 61
EPILOGUE. 91
V. A COVERED BRIDGE AT LUCERNE. 126
VI. THE SCHOOL OF SALERNO. 145
EPILOGUE. 162

THE GOLDEN LEGEND

BY
Henry Wadsworth Longfellow

PROLOGUE.

THE SPIRE OF STRASBURG CATHEDRAL.

Night and storm. LUCIFER, *with the Powers of the Air, trying to tear down the Cross.*

 Lucifer. HASTEN! hasten!
O ye spirits!
From its station drag the ponderous
Cross of iron, that to mock us
Is uplifted high in air!

 Voices. O, we cannot!
For around it
All the Saints and Guardian Angels
Throng in legions to protect it;
They defeat us everywhere!

 The Bells. Laudo Deum verum
    Plebem voco!
    Congrego clerum!

 Lucifer. Lower! lower!

Hover downward!
Seize the loud, vociferous bells, and
Clashing, clanging, to the pavement
Hurl them from their windy tower!

  Voices. All thy thunders
Here are harmless!
For these bells have been anointed,
And baptized with holy water!
They defy our utmost power.

  The Bells. Defunctos ploro!
           Pestem fugo!
           Festa decoro!

  Lucifer. Shake the casements!
Break the painted
Panes that flame with gold and crimson!
Scatter them like leaves of Autumn,
Swept away before the blast!

  Voices. O, we cannot!
The Archangel
Michael flames from every window,
With the sword of fire that drove us
Headlong, out of heaven, aghast!

  The Bells. Funera plango!
           Fulgora frango!
           Sabbata pango!

  Lucifer. Aim your lightnings
At the oaken,

Massive, iron-studded portals!
Sack the house of God, and scatter
Wide the ashes of the dead!

Voices. O, we cannot!
The Apostles
And the Martyrs, wrapped in mantles,
Stand as wardens at the entrance,
Stand as sentinels o'erhead!

The Bells. Excito lentos!
        Dissipo ventos!
        Paco cruentos!

Lucifer. Baffled! baffled!
Inefficient,
Craven spirits! leave this labor
Unto Time, the great Destroyer!
Come away, ere night is gone!

Voices. Onward! onward!
With the night-wind,
Over field and farm and forest,
Lonely homestead, darksome hamlet,
Blighting all we breathe upon!

    (They sweep away. Organ and Gregorian Chant.)

Choir.   Nocte surgentes
           Vig lemus omnes!

I. THE CASTLE OF VAUTSBERG ON THE RHINE.

A chamber in a tower. PRINCE HENRY, *sitting alone, ill and restless.*

Prince Henry. I cannot sleep! my fervid brain
Calls up the vanished Past again,
And throws its misty splendors deep
Into the pallid realms of sleep!
A breath from that far-distant shore
Comes freshening ever more and more,
And wafts o'er intervening seas
Sweet odors from the Hesperides!
A wind, that through the corridor
Just stirs the curtain, and no more,
And, touching the aeolian strings,
Faints with the burden that it brings!
Come back! ye friendships long departed!
That like o'erflowing streamlets started,
And now are dwindled, one by one,
To stony channels in the sun!
Come back! ye friends, whose lives are ended!
Come back, with all that light attended,
Which seemed to darken and decay
When ye arose and went away!
They come, the shapes of joy and woe,

The airy crowds of long-ago,
The dreams and fancies known of yore,
That have been, and shall be no more.
They change the cloisters of the night
Into a garden of delight;
They make the dark and dreary hours
Open and blossom into flowers!
I would not sleep! I love to be
Again in their fair company;
But ere my lips can bid them stay,
They pass and vanish quite away!

Alas! our memories may retrace
Each circumstance of time and place,
Season and scene come back again,
And outward things unchanged remain;
The rest we cannot reinstate;
Ourselves we cannot re-create,
Nor set our souls to the same key
Of the remembered harmony!

Rest! rest! O, give me rest and peace!
The thought of life that ne'er shall cease
Has something in it like despair,
A weight I am too weak to bear!
Sweeter to this afflicted breast
The thought of never-ending rest!
Sweeter the undisturbed and deep
Tranquillity of endless sleep!

(A flash of lightning, out of which LUCIFER *appears, in the garb of a travelling Physician.*)

Lucifer. All hail Prince Henry!

Prince Henry (starting). Who is it speaks?
Who and what are you?

Lucifer. One who seeks
A moment's audience with the Prince.

Prince Henry. When came you in?

Lucifer. A moment since.
I found your study door unlocked,
And thought you answered when I knocked.

Prince Henry. I did not hear you.

Lucifer. You heard the thunder;
It was loud enough to waken the dead.
And it is not a matter of special wonder
That, when God is walking overhead,
You should not have heard my feeble tread.

Prince Henry. What may your wish or purpose be?

Lucifer. Nothing or everything, as it pleases
Your Highness. You behold in me
Only a traveling Physician;
One of the few who have a mission
To cure incurable diseases,
Or those that are called so.

Prince Henry. Can you bring
The dead to life?

Lucifer. Yes; very nearly.
And, what is a wiser and better thing,
Can keep the living from ever needing
Such an unnatural, strange proceeding,
By showing conclusively and clearly
That death is a stupid blunder merely,
And not a necessity of our lives.
My being here is accidental;
The storm, that against your casement drives,
In the little village below waylaid me.
And there I heard, with a secret delight,
Of your maladies physical and mental,
Which neither astonished nor dismayed me.
And I hastened hither, though late in the night,
To proffer my aid!

   Prince Henry (ironically) For this you came!
Ah, how can I ever hope to requite
This honor from one so erudite?

   Lucifer. The honor is mine, or will be when
I have cured your disease.

   Prince Henry. But not till then.

   Lucifer. What is your illness?

   Prince Henry. It has no name.
A smouldering, dull, perpetual flame,
As in a kiln, burns in my veins,
Sending up vapors to the head,
My heart has become a dull lagoon,
Which a kind of leprosy drinks and drains;

I am accounted as one who is dead,
And, indeed, I think that I shall be soon.

Lucifer And has Gordonius the Divine,
In his famous Lily of Medicine,--
I see the book lies open before you,--
No remedy potent enough to restore you?

Prince Henry. None whatever!

Lucifer The dead are dead,
And their oracles dumb, when questioned
Of the new diseases that human life
Evolves in its progress, rank and rife.
Consult the dead upon things that were,
But the living only on things that are.
Have you done this, by the appliance
And aid of doctors?

Prince Henry. Ay, whole schools
Of doctors, with their learned rules,
But the case is quite beyond their science.
Even the doctors of Salern
Send me back word they can discern
No cure for a malady like this,
Save one which in its nature is
Impossible, and cannot be!

Lucifer That sounds oracular!

Prince Henry Unendurable!

Lucifer What is their remedy?

Prince Henry You shall see;
Writ in this scroll is the mystery.

Lucifer (reading). "Not to be cured, yet not incurable!
The only remedy that remains
Is the blood that flows from a maiden's veins,
Who of her own free will shall die,
And give her life as the price of yours!"
That is the strangest of all cures,
And one, I think, you will never try;
The prescription you may well put by,
As something impossible to find
Before the world itself shall end!
And yet who knows? One cannot say
That into some maiden's brain that kind
Of madness will not find its way.
Meanwhile permit me to recommend,
As the matter admits of no delay,
My wonderful Catholicon,
Of very subtile and magical powers!

Prince Henry. Purge with your nostrums and drugs infernal
The spouts and gargoyles of these towers,
Not me! My faith is utterly gone
In every power but the Power Supernal!
Pray tell me, of what school are you?

Lucifer. Both of the Old and of the New!
The school of Hermes Trismegistus,
Who uttered his oracles sublime
Before the Olympiads, in the dew
Of the early dawn and dusk of Time,
The reign of dateless old Hephaestus!

As northward, from its Nubian springs,
The Nile, forever new and old,
Among the living and the dead,
Its mighty, mystic stream has rolled;
So, starting from its fountain-head
Under the lotus-leaves of Isis,
From the dead demigods of eld,
Through long, unbroken lines of kings
Its course the sacred art has held,
Unchecked, unchanged by man's devices.
This art the Arabian Geber taught,
And in alembics, finely wrought,
Distilling herbs and flowers, discovered
The secret that so long had hovered
Upon the misty verge of Truth,
The Elixir of Perpetual Youth,
Called Alcohol, in the Arab speech!
Like him, this wondrous lore I teach!

Prince Henry. What! an adept?

Lucifer. Nor less, nor more!

Prince Henry. I am a reader of such books,
A lover of that mystic lore!
With such a piercing glance it looks
Into great Nature's open eye,
And sees within it trembling lie
The portrait of the Deity!
And yet, alas! with all my pains,
The secret and the mystery
Have baffled and eluded me,
Unseen the grand result remains!

Lucifer (showing a flask). Behold it here! this little flask
Contains the wonderful quintessence,
The perfect flower and efflorescence,
Of all the knowledge man can ask!
Hold it up thus against the light!

Prince Henry. How limpid, pure, and crystalline,
How quick, and tremulous, and bright
The little wavelets dance and shine,
As were it the Water of Life in sooth!

Lucifer. It is! It assuages every pain,
Cures all disease, and gives again
To age the swift delights of youth.
Inhale its fragrance.

Prince Henry. It is sweet.
A thousand different odors meet
And mingle in its rare perfume,
Such as the winds of summer waft
At open windows through a room!

Lucifer. Will you not taste it?

Prince Henry. Will one draught
Suffice?

Lucifer. If not, you can drink more.

Prince Henry. Into this crystal goblet pour
So much as safely I may drink.

Lucifer (pouring). Let not the quantity alarm you:

You may drink all; it will not harm you.

Prince Henry. I am as one who on the brink
Of a dark river stands and sees
The waters flow, the landscape dim
Around him waver, wheel, and swim,
And, ere he plunges, stops to think
Into what whirlpools he may sink;
One moment pauses, and no more,
Then madly plunges from the shore!
Headlong into the dark mysteries
Of life and death I boldly leap,
Nor fear the fateful current's sweep,
Nor what in ambush lurks below!
For death is better than disease!

(An ANGEL *with an aeolian harp hovers in the air*.)

Angel. Woe! woe! eternal woe!
Not only the whispered prayer
Of love,
But the imprecations of hate,
Reverberate
Forever and ever through the air
Above!
This fearful curse
Shakes the great universe!

Lucifer (disappearing). Drink! drink!
And thy soul shall sink
Down into the dark abyss,
Into the infinite abyss,
From which no plummet nor rope

Ever drew up the silver sand of hope!

  Prince Henry (drinking). It is like a draught of fire!
Through every vein
I feel again
The fever of youth, the soft desire;
A rapture that is almost pain
Throbs in my heart and fills my brain!
O joy! O joy! I feel
The band of steel
That so long and heavily has pressed
Upon my breast
Uplifted, and the malediction
Of my affliction
Is taken from me, and my weary breast
At length finds rest.

  The Angel. It is but the rest of the fire, from which the air
              has been taken!
It is but the rest of the sand, when the hour-glass is not shaken!
It is but the rest of the tide between the ebb and the flow!
It is but the rest of the wind between the flaws that blow!
With fiendish laughter,
Hereafter,
This false physician
Will mock thee in thy perdition.

  Prince Henry. Speak! speak!
Who says that I am ill?
I am not ill! I am not weak!
The trance, the swoon, the dream, is o'er!
I feel the chill of death no more!
At length,

I stand renewed in all my strength!
Beneath me I can feel
The great earth stagger and reel,
As it the feet of a descending God
Upon its surface trod,
And like a pebble it rolled beneath his heel!
This, O brave physician! this
Is thy great Palingenesis!

(Drinks again.)

The Angel. Touch the goblet no more!
It will make thy heart sore
To its very core!
Its perfume is the breath
Of the Angel of Death,
And the light that within it lies
Is the flash of his evil eyes.
Beware! O, beware!
For sickness, sorrow, and care
All are there!

Prince Henry (sinking back). O thou voice within my breast!
Why entreat me, why upbraid me,
When the steadfast tongues of truth
And the flattering hopes of youth
Have all deceived me and betrayed me?
Give me, give me rest, O, rest!
Golden visions wave and hover,
Golden vapors, waters streaming,
Landscapes moving, changing, gleaming!
I am like a happy lover
Who illumines life with dreaming!

Brave physician! Rare physician!
Well hast thou fulfilled thy mission!

(His head falls On his book.)

  The Angel (receding). Alas! alas!
Like a vapor the golden vision
Shall fade and pass,
And thou wilt find in thy heart again
Only the blight of pain,
And bitter, bitter, bitter contrition!
COURT-YARD OF THE CASTLE.

HUBERT *standing by the gateway.*

  Hubert. How sad the grand old castle looks!
O'erhead, the unmolested rooks
Upon the turret's windy top
Sit, talking of the farmer's crop;
Here in the court-yard springs the grass,
So few are now the feet that pass;
The stately peacocks, bolder grown,
Come hopping down the steps of stone,
As if the castle were their own;
And I, the poor old seneschal,
Haunt, like a ghost, the banquet-hall.
Alas! the merry guests no more
Crowd through the hospital door;
No eyes with youth and passion shine,
No cheeks glow redder than the wine;
No song, no laugh, no jovial din
Of drinking wassail to the pin;
But all is silent, sad, and drear,

And now the only sounds I hear
Are the hoarse rooks upon the walls,
And horses stamping in their stalls!

(A horn sounds.)

What ho! that merry, sudden blast
Reminds me of the days long past!
And, as of old resounding, grate
The heavy hinges of the gate,
And, clattering loud, with iron clank,
Down goes the sounding bridge of plank,
As if it were in haste to greet
The pressure of a traveler's feet!

(Enter WALTER *the Minnesinger*.)

Walter. How now, my friend! This looks quite lonely!
No banner flying from the walls,
No pages and no seneschals,
No wardens, and one porter only!
Is it you, Hubert?

Hubert. Ah! Master Walter!

Walter. Alas! how forms and faces alter!
I did not know you. You look older!
Your hair has grown much grayer and thinner,
And you stoop a little in the shoulder!

Hubert. Alack! I am a poor old sinner,
And, like these towers, begin to moulder;
And you have been absent many a year!

Walter. How is the Prince?

Hubert. He is not here;
He has been ill: and now has fled.

Walter. Speak it out frankly: say he's dead!
Is it not so?

Hubert. No; if you please;
A strange, mysterious disease
Fell on him with a sudden blight.
Whole hours together he would stand
Upon the terrace, in a dream,
Resting his head upon his hand,
Best pleased when he was most alone,
Like Saint John Nepomuck in stone,
Looking down into a stream.
In the Round Tower, night after night,
He sat, and bleared his eyes with books;
Until one morning we found him there
Stretched on the floor, as if in a swoon
He had fallen from his chair.
We hardly recognized his sweet looks!

Walter. Poor Prince!

Hubert. I think he might have mended;
And he did mend; but very soon
The Priests came flocking in, like rooks,
With all their crosiers and their crooks,
And so at last the matter ended.

Walter. How did it end?

Hubert. Why, in Saint Rochus
They made him stand, and wait his doom;
And, as if he were condemned to the tomb,
Began to mutter their hocus pocus.
First, the Mass for the Dead they chaunted.
Then three times laid upon his head
A shovelful of church-yard clay,
Saying to him, as he stood undaunted,
"This is a sign that thou art dead,
So in thy heart be penitent!"
And forth from the chapel door he went
Into disgrace and banishment,
Clothed in a cloak of hodden gray,
And bearing a wallet, and a bell,
Whose sound should be a perpetual knell
To keep all travelers away.

Walter. O, horrible fate! Outcast, rejected,
As one with pestilence infected!

Hubert. Then was the family tomb unsealed,
And broken helmet, sword and shield,
Buried together, in common wreck,
As is the custom, when the last
Of any princely house has passed,
And thrice, as with a trumpet-blast,
A herald shouted down the stair
The words of warning and despair,--
"O Hoheneck! O Hoheneck!"

Walter. Still in my soul that cry goes on,--
Forever gone! forever gone!
Ah, what a cruel sense of loss,

Like a black shadow, would fall across
The hearts of all, if he should die!
His gracious presence upon earth
Was as a fire upon a hearth;
As pleasant songs, at morning sung,
The words that dropped from his sweet tongue
Strengthened our hearts; or, heard at night,
Made all our slumbers soft and light.
Where is he?

Hubert. In the Odenwald.
Some of his tenants, unappalled
By fear of death, or priestly word,--
A holy family, that make
Each meal a Supper of the Lord,--
Have him beneath their watch and ward,
For love of him, and Jesus' sake!
Pray you come in. For why should I
With outdoor hospitality
My prince's friend thus entertain?

Walter. I would a moment here remain.
But you, good Hubert, go before,
Fill me a goblet of May-drink,
As aromatic as the May
From which it steals the breath away,
And which he loved so well of yore;
It is of him that I would think
You shall attend me, when I call,
In the ancestral banquet hall.
Unseen companions, guests of air,
You cannot wait on, will be there;
They taste not food, they drink not wine,

But their soft eyes look into mine,
And their lips speak to me, and all
The vast and shadowy banquet-hall
Is full of looks and words divine!

(Leaning over the parapet.)

The day is done; and slowly from the scene
The stooping sun upgathers his spent shafts,
And puts them back into his golden quiver!
Below me in the valley, deep and green
As goblets are, from which in thirsty draughts
We drink its wine, the swift and mantling river
Flows on triumphant through these lovely regions,
Etched with the shadows of its sombre margent,
And soft, reflected clouds of gold and argent!
Yes, there it flows, forever, broad and still,
As when the vanguard of the Roman legions
First saw it from the top of yonder hill!
How beautiful it is! Fresh fields of wheat,
Vineyard, and town, and tower with fluttering flag,
The consecrated chapel on the crag,
And the white hamlet gathered round its base,
Like Mary sitting at her Saviour's feet,
And looking up at his beloved face!
O friend! O best of friends! Thy absence more
Than the impending night darkens the landscape o'er!

II.
A FARM IN THE ODENWALD

A garden; morning; PRINCE HENRY *seated, with a book*. ELSIE, *at a distance, gathering flowers.*

Prince Henry (reading). One morning, all alone,
Out of his convent of gray stone,
Into the forest older, darker, grayer,
His lips moving as if in prayer,
His head sunken upon his breast
As in a dream of rest,
Walked the Monk Felix. All about
The broad, sweet sunshine lay without,
Filling the summer air;
And within the woodlands as he trod,
The twilight was like the Truce of God
With worldly woe and care;
Under him lay the golden moss;
And above him the boughs of hemlock-tree
Waved, and made the sign of the cross,
And whispered their Benedicites;
And from the ground
Rose an odor sweet and fragrant
Of the wild flowers and the vagrant
Vines that wandered,

Seeking the sunshine, round and round.
These he heeded not, but pondered
On the volume in his hand,
A volume of Saint Augustine;
Wherein he read of the unseen
Splendors of God's great town
In the unknown land,
And, with his eyes cast down
In humility, he said:
"I believe, O God,
What herein I have read,
But alas! I do not understand!"

And lo! he heard
The sudden singing of a bird,
A snow-white bird, that from a cloud
Dropped down,
And among the branches brown
Sat singing
So sweet, and clear, and loud,
It seemed a thousand harp strings ringing.
And the Monk Felix closed his book,
And long, long,
With rapturous look,
He listened to the song,
And hardly breathed or stirred,
Until he saw, as in a vision,
The land Elysian,
And in the heavenly city heard
Angelic feet
Fall on the golden flagging of the street.
And he would fain
Have caught the wondrous bird,

But strove in vain;
For it flew away, away,
Far over hill and dell,
And instead of its sweet singing
He heard the convent bell
Suddenly in the silence ringing
For the service of noonday.
And he retraced
His pathway homeward sadly and in haste.

In the convent there was a change!
He looked for each well known face,
But the faces were new and strange;
New figures sat in the oaken stalls,
New voices chaunted in the choir,
Yet the place was the same place,
The same dusky walls
Of cold, gray stone,
The same cloisters and belfry and spire.

A stranger and alone
Among that brotherhood
The Monk Felix stood
"Forty years," said a Friar.
"Have I been Prior
Of this convent in the wood,
But for that space
Never have I beheld thy face!"

The heart of the Monk Felix fell:
And he answered with submissive tone,
"This morning, after the hour of Prime,
I left my cell,

And wandered forth alone,
Listening all the time
To the melodious singing
Of a beautiful white bird,
Until I heard
The bells of the convent ringing
Noon from their noisy towers,
It was as if I dreamed;
For what to me had seemed
Moments only, had been hours!"

"Years!" said a voice close by.
It was an aged monk who spoke,
From a bench of oak
Fastened against the wall;--
He was the oldest monk of all.
For a whole century
Had he been there,
Serving God in prayer,
The meekest and humblest of his creatures.
He remembered well the features
Of Felix, and he said,
Speaking distinct and slow:
"One hundred years ago,
When I was a novice in this place,
There was here a monk, full of God's grace,
Who bore the name
Of Felix, and this man must be the same."

And straightway
They brought forth to the light of day
A volume old and brown,
A huge tome, bound

With brass and wild-boar's hide,
Therein were written down
The names of all who had died
In the convent, since it was edified.
And there they found,
Just as the old monk said,
That on a certain day and date,
One hundred years before,
Had gone forth from the convent gate
The Monk Felix, and never more
Had entered that sacred door.
He had been counted among the dead!
And they knew, at last,
That, such had been the power
Of that celestial and immortal song,
A hundred years had passed,
And had not seemed so long
As a single hour!

(ELSIE *comes in with flowers.*)

Elsie. Here are flowers for you,
But they are not all for you.
Some of them are for the Virgin
And for Saint Cecilia.

Prince Henry. As thou standest there,
Thou seemest to me like the angel
That brought the immortal roses
To Saint Cecilia's bridal chamber.

Elsie. But these will fade.

Prince Henry. Themselves will fade,
But not their memory,
And memory has the power
To re-create them from the dust.
They remind me, too,
Of martyred Dorothea,
Who from celestial gardens sent
Flowers as her witnesses
To him who scoffed and doubted.

Elsie. Do you know the story
Of Christ and the Sultan's daughter?
That is the prettiest legend of them all.

Prince Henry. Then tell it to me.
But first come hither.
Lay the flowers down beside me.
And put both thy hands in mine.
Now tell me the story.

Elsie. Early in the morning
The Sultan's daughter
Walked in her father's garden,
Gathering the bright flowers,
All full of dew.

Prince Henry. Just as thou hast been doing
This morning, dearest Elsie.

Elsie. And as she gathered them,
She wondered more and more
Who was the Master of the Flowers,
And made them grow

Out of the cold, dark earth.
"In my heart," she said,
"I love him; and for him
Would leave my father's palace,
To labor in his garden."

Prince Henry. Dear, innocent child!
How sweetly thou recallest
The long-forgotten legend,
That in my early childhood
My mother told me!
Upon my brain
It reappears once more,
As a birth-mark on the forehead
When a hand suddenly
Is laid upon it, and removed!

Elsie. And at midnight,
As she lay upon her bed,
She heard a voice
Call to her from the garden,
And, looking forth from her window,
She saw a beautiful youth
Standing among the flowers.
It was the Lord Jesus;
And she went down to him,
And opened the door for him;
And he said to her, "O maiden!
Thou hast thought of me with love,
And for thy sake
Out of my Father's kingdom
Have I come hither:
I am the Master of the Flowers.

My garden is in Paradise,
And if thou wilt go with me,
Thy bridal garland
Shall be of bright red flowers."
And then he took from his finger
A golden ring,
And asked the Sultan's daughter
If she would be his bride.
And when she answered him with love,
His wounds began to bleed,
And she said to him,
"O Love! how red thy heart is,
And thy hands are full of roses,"
"For thy sake," answered he,
"For thy sake is my heart so red,
For thee I bring these roses.
I gathered them at the cross
Whereon I died for thee!
Come, for my Father calls.
Thou art my elected bride!"
And the Sultan's daughter
Followed him to his Father's garden.

Prince Henry. Wouldst thou have done so, Elsie?

Elsie. Yes, very gladly.

Prince Henry. Then the Celestial Bridegroom
Will come for thee also.
Upon thy forehead he will place,
Not his crown of thorns,
But a crown of roses.
In thy bridal chamber,

Like Saint Cecilia,
Thou shall hear sweet music,
And breathe the fragrance
Of flowers immortal!
Go now and place these flowers
Before her picture.

A ROOM IN THE FARM-HOUSE.

Twilight. URSULA *spinning.* GOTTLIEB *asleep in his chair.*

Ursula. Darker and darker! Hardly a glimmer
Of light comes in at the window-pane;
Or is it my eyes are growing dimmer?
I cannot disentangle this skein,
Nor wind it rightly upon the reel.
Elsie!

Gottlieb (starting). The stopping of thy wheel
Has wakened me out of a pleasant dream.
I thought I was sitting beside a stream,
And heard the grinding of a mill,
When suddenly the wheels stood still,
And a voice cried "Elsie" in my ear!
It startled me, it seemed so near.

Ursula. I was calling her: I want a light.
I cannot see to spin my flax.
Bring the lamp, Elsie. Dost thou hear?

Elsie (within). In a moment!

Gottlieb. Where are Bertha and Max?

Ursula. They are sitting with Elsie at the door.
She is telling them stories of the wood,
And the Wolf, and Little Red Ridinghood.

Gottlieb. And where is the Prince?

Ursula. In his room overhead;
I heard him walking across the floor,
As he always does, with a heavy tread.

(ELSIE *comes in with a lamp.* MAX *and* BERTHA *follow her; and they all sing the Evening Song on the lighting of the lamps.*)

EVENING SONG.

O gladsome light
Of the Father Immortal,
And of the celestial
Sacred and blessed
Jesus, our Saviour!

Now to the sunset
Again hast thou brought us;
And, seeing the evening
Twilight, we bless thee,
Praise thee, adore thee!

Father omnipotent!
Son, the Life-giver!
Spirit, the Comforter!

Worthy at all times
Of worship and wonder!

Prince Henry (at the door). Amen!

Ursula. Who was it said Amen?

Elsie. It was the Prince: he stood at the door,
And listened a moment, as we chaunted
The evening song. He is gone again.
I have often seen him there before.

Ursula. Poor Prince!

Gottlieb. I thought the house was haunted!
Poor Prince, alas! and yet as mild
And patient as the gentlest child!

Max. I love him because he is so good,
And makes me such fine bows and arrows,
To shoot at the robins and the sparrows,
And the red squirrels in the wood!

Bertha. I love him, too!

Gottlieb. Ah, yes! we all
Love him, from the bottom of our hearts;
He gave us the farm, the house, and the grange,
He gave us the horses and the carts,
And the great oxen in the stall,
The vineyard, and the forest range!
We have nothing to give him but our love!

Bertha. Did he give us the beautiful stork above
On the chimney-top, with its large, round nest?

Gottlieb. No, not the stork; by God in heaven,
As a blessing, the dear, white stork was given;
But the Prince has given us all the rest.
God bless him, and make him well again.

Elsie. Would I could do something for his sake,
Something to cure his sorrow and pain!

Gottlieb. That no one can; neither thou nor I,
Nor any one else.

Elsie. And must he die?

Ursula. Yes; if the dear God does not take
Pity upon him, in his distress,
And work a miracle!

Gottlieb. Or unless
Some maiden, of her own accord,
Offers her life for that of her lord,
And is willing to die in his stead.

Elsie. I will!

Ursula. Prithee, thou foolish child, be still!
Thou shouldst not say what thou dost not mean!

Elsie. I mean it truly!

Max. O father! this morning,
Down by the mill, in the ravine,
Hans killed a wolf, the very same
That in the night to the sheepfold came,
And ate up my lamb, that was left outside.

Gottlieb. I am glad he is dead. It will be a warning
To the wolves in the forest, far and wide.

Max. And I am going to have his hide!

Bertha. I wonder if this is the wolf that ate
Little Red Ridinghood!

Ursula. O, no!
That wolf was killed a long while ago.
Come, children, it is growing late.

Max. Ah, how I wish I were a man,
As stout as Hans is, and as strong!
I would do nothing else, the whole day long,
But just kill wolves.

Gottlieb. Then go to bed,
And grow as fast as a little boy can.
Bertha is half asleep already.
See how she nods her heavy head,
And her sleepy feet are so unsteady
She will hardly be able to creep upstairs.

Ursula. Good-night, my children. Here's the light.
And do not forget to say your prayers
Before you sleep.

Gottlieb. Good-night!

Max and Bertha. Good-night!

(They go out with ELSIE.)

Ursula, (spinning). She is a strange and wayward child,
That Elsie of ours. She looks so old,
And thoughts and fancies weird and wild
Seem of late to have taken hold
Of her heart, that was once so docile and mild!

Gottlieb. She is like all girls.

Ursula. Ah no, forsooth!
Unlike all I have ever seen.
For she has visions and strange dreams,
And in all her words and ways, she seems
Much older than she is in truth.
Who would think her but fourteen?
And there has been of late such a change!
My heart is heavy with fear and doubt
That she may not live till the year is out.
She is so strange,--so strange,--so strange!

Gottlieb. I am not troubled with any such fear!
She will live and thrive for many a year.
ELSIE'S CHAMBER.
Night. ELSIE *praying.*

Elsie. My Redeemer and my Lord,
I beseech thee, I entreat thee,
Guide me in each act and word,

That hereafter I may meet thee,
Watching, waiting, hoping, yearning,
With my lamp well trimmed and burning!

Interceding
With these bleeding
Wounds upon thy hands and side,
For all who have lived and erred
Thou hast suffered, thou hast died,
Scourged, and mocked, and crucified,
And in the grave hast thou been buried!

If my feeble prayer can reach thee,
O my Saviour, I beseech thee,
Even as thou hast died for me,
More sincerely
Let me follow where thou leadest,
Let me, bleeding as thou bleedest,
Die, if dying I may give
Life to one who asks to live,
And more nearly,
Dying thus, resemble thee!

THE CHAMBER OF GOTTLIEB AND URSULA.
Midnight. ELSIE *standing by their bedside, weeping.*

Gottlieb. The wind is roaring; the rushing rain
Is loud upon roof and window-pane,
As if the Wild Huntsman of Rodenstein,
Boding evil to me and mine,
Were abroad to-night with his ghostly train!
In the brief lulls of the tempest wild,
The dogs howl in the yard; and hark!

Some one is sobbing in the dark,
Here in the chamber!

Elsie. It is I.

Ursula. Elsie! what ails thee, my poor child?

Elsie. I am disturbed and much distressed,
In thinking our dear Prince must die,
I cannot close mine eyes, nor rest.

Gottlieb. What wouldst thou? In the Power Divine
His healing lies, not in our own;
It is in the hand of God alone.

Elsie. Nay, he has put it into mine,
And into my heart!

Gottlieb. Thy words are wild!

Ursula. What dost thou mean? my child! my child!

Elsie. That for our dear Prince Henry's sake
I will myself the offering make,
And give my life to purchase his.

Ursula Am I still dreaming, or awake?
Thou speakest carelessly of death,
And yet thou knowest not what it is.

Elsie. 'T is the cessation of our breath.
Silent and motionless we lie;

And no one knoweth more than this.
I saw our little Gertrude die,
She left off breathing, and no more
I smoothed the pillow beneath her head.
She was more beautiful than before.
Like violets faded were her eyes;
By this we knew that she was dead.
Through the open window looked the skies
Into the chamber where she lay,
And the wind was like the sound of wings,
As if angels came to bear her away.
Ah! when I saw and felt these things,
I found it difficult to stay;
I longed to die, as she had died,
And go forth with her, side by side.
The Saints are dead, the Martyrs dead,
And Mary, and our Lord, and I
Would follow in humility
The way by them illumined!

Ursula. My child! my child! thou must not die!

Elsie Why should I live? Do I not know
The life of woman is full of woe?
Toiling on and on and on,
With breaking heart, and tearful eyes,
And silent lips, and in the soul
The secret longings that arise,
Which this world never satisfies!
Some more, some less, but of the whole
Not one quite happy, no, not one!

Ursula. It is the malediction of Eve!

Elsie. In place of it, let me receive
The benediction of Mary, then.

Gottlieb. Ah, woe is me! Ah, woe is me!
Most wretched am I among men!

Ursula. Alas! that I should live to see
Thy death, beloved, and to stand
Above thy grave! Ah, woe the day!

Elsie. Thou wilt not see it. I shall lie
Beneath the flowers of another land,
For at Salerno, far away
Over the mountains, over the sea,
It is appointed me to die!
And it will seem no more to thee
Than if at the village on market-day
I should a little longer stay
Than I am used.

Ursula. Even as thou sayest!
And how my heart beats, when thou stayest!
I cannot rest until my sight
Is satisfied with seeing thee.
What, then, if thou wert dead?

Gottlieb Ah me!
Of our old eyes thou art the light!
The joy of our old hearts art thou!
And wilt thou die?

Ursula. Not now! not now!

Elsie Christ died for me, and shall not I
Be willing for my Prince to die?
You both are silent; you cannot speak.
This said I, at our Saviour's feast,
After confession, to the priest,
And even he made no reply.
Does he not warn us all to seek
The happier, better land on high,
Where flowers immortal never wither,
And could he forbid me to go thither?

Gottlieb. In God's own time, my heart's delight!
When he shall call thee, not before!

Elsie. I heard him call. When Christ ascended
Triumphantly, from star to star,
He left the gates of heaven ajar.
I had a vision in the night,
And saw him standing at the door
Of his Father's mansion, vast and splendid,
And beckoning to me from afar.
I cannot stay!

Gottlieb. She speaks almost
As if it were the Holy Ghost
Spake through her lips, and in her stead!
What if this were of God?

Ursula. Ah, then
Gainsay it dare we not.

Gottlieb. Amen!
Elsie! the words that thou hast said

Are strange and new for us to hear,
And fill our hearts with doubt and fear.
Whether it be a dark temptation
Of the Evil One, or God's inspiration,
We in our blindness cannot say.
We must think upon it, and pray;
For evil and good in both resembles.
If it be of God, his will be done!
May he guard us from the Evil One!
How hot thy hand is! how it trembles!
Go to thy bed, and try to sleep.

  Ursula. Kiss me. Good-night; and do not weep!

    (ELSIE *goes out.*)

Ah, what an awful thing is this!
I almost shuddered at her kiss.
As if a ghost had touched my cheek,
I am so childish and so weak!
As soon as I see the earliest gray
Of morning glimmer in the east,
I will go over to the priest,
And hear what the good man has to say!
A VILLAGE CHURCH.
A woman kneeling at the confessional.

  The Parish Priest (from within). Go, sin no more! Thy penance o'er,
A new and better life begin!
God maketh thee forever free
From the dominion of thy sin!
Go, sin no more! He will restore

The peace that filled thy heart before,
And pardon thine iniquity!

(The woman goes out. The Priest comes forth, and
  walks slowly up and down the church.)

O blessed Lord! how much I need
Thy light to guide me on my way!
So many hands, that, without heed,
Still touch thy wounds, and make them bleed!
So many feet, that, day by day,
Still wander from thy fold astray!
Unless thou fill me with thy light,
I cannot lead thy flock aright;
Nor, without thy support, can bear
The burden of so great a care,
But am myself a castaway!

    (A pause.)

The day is drawing to its close;
And what good deeds, since first it rose,
Have I presented, Lord, to thee,
As offerings of my ministry?
What wrong repressed, what right maintained
What struggle passed, what victory gained,
What good attempted and attained?
Feeble, at best, is my endeavor!
I see, but cannot reach, the height
That lies forever in the light,
And yet forever and forever,
When seeming just within my grasp,
I feel my feeble hands unclasp,

And sink discouraged into night!
For thine own purpose, thou hast sent
The strife and the discouragement!

    (A pause.)

Why stayest thou, Prince of Hoheneck?
Why keep me pacing to and fro
Amid these aisles of sacred gloom,
Counting my footsteps as I go,
And marking with each step a tomb?
Why should the world for thee make room,
And wait thy leisure and thy beck?
Thou comest in the hope to hear
Some word of comfort and of cheer.
What can I say? I cannot give
The counsel to do this and live;
But rather, firmly to deny
The tempter, though his power is strong,
And, inaccessible to wrong,
Still like a martyr live and die!

    (A pause.)

The evening air grows dusk and brown;
I must go forth into the town,
To visit beds of pain and death,
Of restless limbs, and quivering breath,
And sorrowing hearts, and patient eyes
That see, through tears, the sun go down,
But never more shall see it rise.
The poor in body and estate,
The sick and the disconsolate.

Must not on man's convenience wait.

(Goes out. Enter LUCIFER, ***as a Priest***. LUCIFER, ***with a genuflexion, mocking***.)

This is the Black Pater-noster.
God was my foster,
He fostered me
Under the book of the Palm-tree!
St. Michael was my dame.
He was born at Bethlehem,
He was made of flesh and blood.
God send me my right food,
My right food, and shelter too,
That I may to yon kirk go,
To read upon yon sweet book
Which the mighty God of heaven shook.
Open, open, hell's gates!
Shut, shut, heaven's gates!
All the devils in the air
The stronger be, that hear the Black Prayer!

(Looking round the church.)

What a darksome and dismal place!
I wonder that any man has the face
To call such a hole the House of the Lord,
And the Gate of Heaven,--yet such is the word.
Ceiling, and walls, and windows old,
Covered with cobwebs, blackened with mould;
Dust on the pulpit, dust on the stairs,
Dust on the benches, and stalls, and chairs!
The pulpit, from which such ponderous sermons

Have fallen down on the brains of the Germans,
With about as much real edification
As if a great Bible, bound in lead,
Had fallen, and struck them on the head;
And I ought to remember that sensation!
Here stands the holy water stoup!
Holy-water it may be to many,
But to me, the veriest Liquor Gehennae!
It smells like a filthy fast day soup!
Near it stands the box for the poor;
With its iron padlock, safe and sure,
I and the priest of the parish know
Whither all these charities go;
Therefore, to keep up the institution,
I will add my little contribution!

(He puts in money.)

Underneath this mouldering tomb,
With statue of stone, and scutcheon of brass,
Slumbers a great lord of the village.
All his life was riot and pillage,
But at length, to escape the threatened doom
Of the everlasting, penal fire,
He died in the dress of a mendicant friar,
And bartered his wealth for a daily mass.
But all that afterward came to pass,
And whether he finds it dull or pleasant,
Is kept a secret for the present,
At his own particular desire.

And here, in a corner of the wall,
Shadowy, silent, apart from all,

The Golden Legend

With its awful portal open wide,
And its latticed windows on either side,
And its step well worn by the bended knees
Of one or two pious centuries,
Stands the village confessional!
Within it, as an honored guest,
I will sit me down awhile and rest!

(Seats himself in the confessional.)

Here sits the priest, and faint and low,
Like the sighing of an evening breeze,
Comes through these painted lattices
The ceaseless sound of human woe,
Here, while her bosom aches and throbs
With deep and agonizing sobs,
That half are passion, half contrition,
The luckless daughter of perdition
Slowly confesses her secret shame!
The time, the place, the lover's name!
Here the grim murderer, with a groan,
From his bruised conscience rolls the stone,
Thinking that thus he can atone
For ravages of sword and flame!
Indeed, I marvel, and marvel greatly,
How a priest can sit here so sedately,
Reading, the whole year out and in,
Naught but the catalogue of sin,
And still keep any faith whatever
In human virtue! Never! never!

I cannot repeat a thousandth part
Of the horrors and crimes and sins and woes

That arise, when with palpitating throes
The graveyard in the human heart
Gives up its dead, at the voice of the priest,
As if he were an archangel, at least.
It makes a peculiar atmosphere,
This odor of earthly passions and crimes,
Such as I like to breathe, at times,
And such as often brings me here
In the hottest and most pestilential season.
To-day, I come for another reason;
To foster and ripen an evil thought
In a heart that is almost to madness wrought,
And to make a murderer out of a prince,
A sleight of hand I learned long since!
He comes In the twilight he will not see
the difference between his priest and me!
In the same net was the mother caught!

(Prince Henry entering and kneeling at the confessional.)

Remorseful, penitent, and lowly,
I come to crave, O Father holy,
Thy benediction on my head.

Lucifer. The benediction shall be said
After confession, not before!
'T is a God speed to the parting guest,
Who stands already at the door,
Sandalled with holiness, and dressed
In garments pure from earthly stain.
Meanwhile, hast thou searched well thy breast?
Does the same madness fill thy brain?
Or have thy passion and unrest

Vanished forever from thy mind?

Prince Henry. By the same madness still made blind,
By the same passion still possessed,
I come again to the house of prayer,
A man afflicted and distressed!
As in a cloudy atmosphere,
Through unseen sluices of the air,
A sudden and impetuous wind
Strikes the great forest white with fear,
And every branch, and bough, and spray
Points all its quivering leaves one way,
And meadows of grass, and fields of grain,
And the clouds above, and the slanting rain,
And smoke from chimneys of the town,
Yield themselves to it, and bow down,
So does this dreadful purpose press
Onward, with irresistible stress,
And all my thoughts and faculties,
Struck level by the strength of this,
From their true inclination turn,
And all stream forward to Salem!

Lucifer. Alas! we are but eddies of dust,
Uplifted by the blast, and whirled
Along the highway of the world
A moment only, then to fall
Back to a common level all,
At the subsiding of the gust!

Prince Henry. O holy Father! pardon in me
The oscillation of a mind
Unsteadfast, and that cannot find

Its centre of rest and harmony!
For evermore before mine eyes
This ghastly phantom flits and flies,
And as a madman through a crowd,
With frantic gestures and wild cries,
It hurries onward, and aloud
Repeats its awful prophecies!
Weakness is wretchedness! To be strong
Is to be happy! I am weak,
And cannot find the good I seek,
Because I feel and fear the wrong!

Lucifer. Be not alarmed! The Church is kind--
And in her mercy and her meekness
She meets half-way her children's weakness,
Writes their transgressions in the dust!
Though in the Decalogue we find
The mandate written, "Thou shalt not kill!"
Yet there are cases when we must.
In war, for instance, or from scathe
To guard and keep the one true Faith!
We must look at the Decalogue in the light
Of an ancient statute, that was meant
For a mild and general application,
To be understood with the reservation,
That, in certain instances, the Right
Must yield to the Expedient!
Thou art a Prince. If thou shouldst die,
What hearts and hopes would prostrate he!
What noble deeds, what fair renown,
Into the grave with thee go down!
What acts of valor and courtesy
Remain undone, and die with thee!

The Golden Legend

Thou art the last of all thy race!
With thee a noble name expires,
And vanishes from the earth's face
The glorious memory of thy sires!
She is a peasant. In her veins
Flows common and plebeian blood;
It is such as daily and hourly stains
The dust and the turf of battle plains,
By vassals shed, in a crimson flood,
Without reserve, and without reward,
At the slightest summons of their lord!
But thine is precious, the fore-appointed
Blood of kings, of God's anointed!
Moreover, what has the world in store
For one like her, but tears and toil?
Daughter of sorrow, serf of the soil,
A peasant's child and a peasant's wife,
And her soul within her sick and sore
With the roughness and barrenness of life!
I marvel not at the heart's recoil
From a fate like this, in one so tender,
Nor at its eagerness to surrender
All the wretchedness, want, and woe
That await it in this world below,
For the unutterable splendor
Of the world of rest beyond the skies.
So the Church sanctions the sacrifice:
Therefore inhale this healing balm,
And breathe this fresh life into thine;
Accept the comfort and the calm
She offers, as a gift divine,
Let her fall down and anoint thy feet
With the ointment costly and most sweet

Of her young blood, and thou shall live.

Prince Henry. And will the righteous Heaven forgive?
No action, whether foul or fair,
Is ever done, but it leaves somewhere
A record, written by fingers ghostly,
As a blessing or a curse, and mostly
In the greater weakness or greater strength
Of the acts which follow it, till at length
The wrongs of ages are redressed,
And the justice of God made manifest!

Lucifer In ancient records it is stated
That, whenever an evil deed is done,
Another devil is created
To scourge and torment the offending one!
But evil is only good perverted,
And Lucifer, the Bearer of Light,
But an angel fallen and deserted,
Thrust from his Father's house with a curse
Into the black and endless night.

Prince Henry. If justice rules the universe,
From the good actions of good men
Angels of light should be begotten,
And thus the balance restored again.

Lucifer. Yes; if the world were not so rotten,
And so given over to the Devil!

Prince Henry. But this deed, is it good or evil?
Have I thine absolution free
To do it, and without restriction?

Lucifer. Ay; and from whatsoever sin
Lieth around it and within,
From all crimes in which it may involve thee,
I now release thee and absolve thee!

Prince Henry. Give me thy holy benediction.

Lucifer. (stretching forth his hand and muttering),
    Maledictione perpetua
    Maledicat vos
    Pater eternus!

The Angel (with the aeolian harp). Take heed! take heed!
Noble art thou in thy birth,
By the good and the great of earth
Hast thou been taught!
Be noble in every thought
And in every deed!
Let not the illusion of thy senses
Betray thee to deadly offences.
Be strong! be good! be pure!
The right only shall endure,
All things else are but false pretences!
I entreat thee, I implore,
Listen no more
To the suggestions of an evil spirit,
That even now is there,
Making the foul seem fair,
And selfishness itself a virtue and a merit!

A ROOM IN THE FARM-HOUSE.

Gottlieb. It is decided! For many days,

And nights as many, we have had
A nameless terror in our breast,
Making us timid, and afraid
Of God, and his mysterious ways!
We have been sorrowful and sad;
Much have we suffered, much have prayed
That he would lead us as is best,
And show us what his will required.
It is decided; and we give
Our child, O Prince, that you may live!

Ursula. It is of God. He has inspired
This purpose in her; and through pain,
Out of a world of sin and woe,
He takes her to himself again.
The mother's heart resists no longer;
With the Angel of the Lord in vain
It wrestled, for he was the stronger.

Gottlieb. As Abraham offered long ago
His son unto the Lord, and even
The Everlasting Father in heaven
Gave his, as a lamb unto the slaughter,
So do I offer up my daughter!

(URSULA *hides her face*.)

Elsie. My life is little,
Only a cup of water,
But pure and limpid.
Take it, O my Prince!
Let it refresh you,
Let it restore you.

It is given willingly,
It is given freely;
May God bless the gift!

Prince Henry. And the giver!

Gottlieb. Amen!

Prince Henry. I accept it!

Gottlieb. Where are the children?

Ursula. They are already asleep.

Gottlieb. What if they were dead?
IN THE GARDEN.
   Elsie. I have one thing to ask of you.

Prince Henry. What is it?
It is already granted.

Elsie. Promise me,
When we are gone from here, and on our way
Are journeying to Salerno, you will not,
By word or deed, endeavor to dissuade me
And turn me from my purpose, but remember
That as a pilgrim to the Holy City
Walks unmolested, and with thoughts of pardon
Occupied wholly, so would I approach
The gates of Heaven, in this great jubilee,
With my petition, putting off from me
All thoughts of earth, as shoes from off my feet.
Promise me this.

Prince Henry. Thy words fall from thy lips
Like roses from the lips of Angelo: and angels
Might stoop to pick them up!

Elsie. Will you not promise?

Prince Henry. If ever we depart upon this journey,
So long to one or both of us, I promise.

Elsie. Shall we not go, then? Have you lifted me
Into the air, only to hurl me back
Wounded upon the ground? and offered me
The waters of eternal life, to bid me
Drink the polluted puddles of this world?

Prince Henry. O Elsie! what a lesson thou dost teach me!
The life which is, and that which is to come,
Suspended hang in such nice equipoise
A breath disturbs the balance; and that scale
In which we throw our hearts preponderates,
And the other, like an empty one, flies up,
And is accounted vanity and air!
To me the thought of death is terrible,
Having such hold on life. To thee it is not
So much even as the lifting of a latch;
Only a step into the open air
Out of a tent already luminous
With light that shines through its transparent walls!
O pure in heart! from thy sweet dust shall grow
Lilies, upon whose petals will be written
"Ave Maria" in characters of gold!

III. A STREET IN STRASBURG.

Night. PRINCE HENRY *wandering alone, wrapped in a cloak.*

Prince Henry. Still is the night. The sound of feet
Has died away from the empty street,
And like an artisan, bending down
His head on his anvil, the dark town
Sleeps, with a slumber deep and sweet.
Sleepless and restless, I alone,
In the dusk and damp of these wails of stone,
Wander and weep in my remorse!

Crier of the dead (ringing a bell). Wake! wake!
All ye that sleep!
Pray for the Dead!
Pray for the Dead!

Prince Henry. Hark! with what accents loud and hoarse
This warder on the walls of death
Sends forth the challenge of his breath!
I see the dead that sleep in the grave!
They rise up and their garments wave,
Dimly and spectral, as they rise,
With the light of another world in their eyes!

Crier of the dead. Wake! wake!
                All ye that sleep!
                Pray for the Dead!
                Pray for the Dead!

Prince Henry. Why for the dead, who are at rest?
Pray for the living, in whose breast
The struggle between right and wrong
Is raging terrible and strong,
As when good angels war with devils!
This is the Master of the Revels,
Who, at Life's flowing feast, proposes
The health of absent friends, and pledges,
Not in bright goblets crowned with roses,
And tinkling as we touch their edges,
But with his dismal, tinkling bell,
That mocks and mimics their funeral knell!

Crier of the dead. Wake! wake!
                All ye that sleep!
                Pray for the Dead!
                Pray for the Dead!

Prince Henry. Wake not, beloved! be thy sleep
Silent as night is, and as deep!
There walks a sentinel at thy gate
Whose heart is heavy and desolate,
And the heavings of whose bosom number
The respirations of thy slumber,
As if some strange, mysterious fate
Had linked two hearts in one, and mine
Went madly wheeling about thine,
Only with wider and wilder sweep!

Crier of the dead (at a distance). Wake! wake!
>All ye that sleep!
>Pray for the Dead!
>Pray for the Dead!

Prince Henry. Lo! with what depth of blackness thrown
Against the clouds, far up the skies,
The walls of the cathedral rise,
Like a mysterious grove of stone,
With fitful lights and shadows bleeding,
As from behind, the moon, ascending,
Lights its dim aisles and paths unknown!
The wind is rising; but the boughs
Rise not and fall not with the wind
That through their foliage sobs and soughs;
Only the cloudy rack behind,
Drifting onward, wild and ragged,
Gives to each spire and buttress jagged
A seeming motion undefined.
Below on the square, an armed knight,
Still as a statue and as white,
Sits on his steed, and the moonbeams quiver
Upon the points of his armor bright
As on the ripples of a river.
He lifts the visor from his cheek,
And beckons, and makes as he would speak.

Walter the Minnesinger Friend! can you tell me where alight
Thuringia's horsemen for the night?
For I have lingered in the rear,
And wander vainly up and down.

Prince Henry I am a stranger in the town,
As thou art, but the voice I hear
Is not a stranger to mine ear.
Thou art Walter of the Vogelweid!

Walter Thou hast guessed rightly; and thy name
Is Henry of Hoheneck!

Prince Henry Ay, the same.

Walter (embracing him). Come closer, closer to my side!
What brings thee hither? What potent charm
Has drawn thee from thy German farm
Into the old Alsatian city?

Prince Henry. A tale of wonder and of pity!
A wretched man, almost by stealth
Dragging my body to Salern,
In the vain hope and search for health,
And destined never to return.
Already thou hast heard the rest
But what brings thee, thus armed and dight
In the equipments of a knight?

Walter. Dost thou not see upon my breast
The cross of the Crusaders shine?
My pathway leads to Palestine.

Prince Henry. Ah, would that way were also mine!
O noble poet! thou whose heart
Is like a nest of singing birds
Rocked on the topmost bough of life,
Wilt thou, too, from our sky depart,

And in the clangor of the strife
Mingle the music of thy words?

Walter. My hopes are high, my heart is proud,
And like a trumpet long and loud,
Thither my thoughts all clang and ring!
My life is in my hand, and lo!
I grasp and bend it as a bow,
And shoot forth from its trembling string
An arrow, that shall be, perchance,
Like the arrow of the Israelite king
Shot from the window toward the east,
That of the Lord's deliverance!

Prince Henry. My life, alas! is what thou seest!
O enviable fate! to be
Strong, beautiful, and armed like thee
With lyre and sword, with song and steel;
A hand to smite, a heart to feel!
Thy heart, thy hand, thy lyre, thy sword,
Thou givest all unto thy Lord,
While I, so mean and abject grown,
Am thinking of myself alone.

Walter. Be patient: Time will reinstate
Thy health and fortunes.

Prince Henry. 'T is too late!
I cannot strive against my fate!

Walter. Come with me; for my steed is weary;
Our journey has been long and dreary,
And, dreaming of his stall, he dints

With his impatient hoofs the flints.

Prince Henry (aside). I am ashamed, in my disgrace,
To look into that noble face!
To-morrow, Walter, let it be.

Walter. To-morrow, at the dawn of day,
I shall again be on my way
Come with me to the hostelry,
For I have many things to say.
Our journey into Italy
Perchance together we may make;
Wilt thou not do it for my sake?

Prince Henry. A sick man's pace would but impede
Thine eager and impatient speed.
Besides, my pathway leads me round
To Hirsehau, in the forest's bound,
Where I assemble man and steed,
And all things for my journey's need.

(They go out. LUCIFER, *flying over the city*.)

Sleep, sleep, O city! till the light
Wakes you to sin and crime again,
Whilst on your dreams, like dismal rain,
I scatter downward through the night
My maledictions dark and deep.
I have more martyrs in your walls
Than God has; and they cannot sleep;
They are my bondsmen and my thralls;
Their wretched lives are full of pain,
Wild agonies of nerve and brain;

And every heart-beat, every breath,
Is a convulsion worse than death!
Sleep, sleep, O city! though within
The circuit of your walls there lies
No habitation free from sin,
And all its nameless miseries;
The aching heart, the aching head,
Grief for the living and the dead,
And foul corruption of the time,
Disease, distress, and want, and woe,
And crimes, and passions that may grow
Until they ripen into, crime!

SQUARE IN FRONT OF THE CATHEDRAL.

Easter Sunday. FRIAR CUTHBERT *preaching to the crowd from a pulpit in the open air*. PRINCE HENRY *and* ELSIE *crossing the square*.

Prince Henry. This is the day, when from the dead
Our Lord arose; and everywhere,
Out of their darkness and despair,
Triumphant over fears and foes,
The hearts of his disciples rose,
When to the women, standing near,
The Angel in shining vesture said,
"The Lord is risen; he is not here!"
And, mindful that the day is come,
On all the hearths in Christendom
The fires are quenched, to be again
Rekindled from the sun, that high
Is dancing in the cloudless sky.

The churches are all decked with flowers.
The salutations among men
Are but the Angel's words divine,
"Christ is arisen!" and the bells
Catch the glad murmur, as it swells,
And chaunt together in their towers.
All hearts are glad; and free from care
The faces of the people shine.
See what a crowd is in the square,
Gaily and gallantly arrayed!

Elsie. Let us go back; I am afraid!

Prince Henry. Nay, let us mount the church-steps here,
Under the doorway's sacred shadow;
We can see all things, and be freer
From the crowd that madly heaves and presses!

Elsie. What a gay pageant! what bright dresses!
It looks like a flower besprinkled meadow.
What is that yonder on the square?

Prince Henry A pulpit in the open air,
And a Friar, who is preaching to the crowd
With a voice so deep and clear and loud,
That, if we listen, and give heed,
His lowest words will reach the ear.

Friar Cuthbert (gesticulating and cracking a postilion's whip) What ho! good people! do you not hear?
Dashing along at the top of his speed,
Booted and spurred, on his jaded steed,
A courier comes with words of cheer.

Courier! what is the news, I pray?
"Christ is arisen!" Whence come you? "From court."
Then I do not believe it; you say it in sport.

    (Cracks his whip again.)

There comes another, riding this way;
We soon shall know what he has to say.
Courier! what are the tidings to-day?
"Christ is arisen!" Whence come you? "From town."
Then I do not believe it; away with you, clown.

    (Cracks his whip more violently.)

And here comes a third, who is spurring amain;
What news do you bring, with your loose-hanging rein,
Your spurs wet with blood, and your bridle with foam?
"Christ is arisen!" Whence come you? "From Rome."
Ah, now I believe. He is risen, indeed.
Ride on with the news, at the top of your speed!

    (Great applause among the crowd.)

To come back to my text! When the news was first spread
That Christ was arisen indeed from the dead,
Very great was the joy of the angels in heaven;
And as great the dispute as to who should carry
The tidings, thereof to the Virgin Mary,
Pierced to the heart with sorrows seven.
Old Father Adam was first to propose,
As being the author of all our woes;
But he was refused, for fear, said they,
He would stop to eat apples on the way!

Abel came next, but petitioned in vain,
Because he might meet with his brother Cain!
Noah, too, was refused, lest his weakness for wine
Should delay him at every tavern sign;
And John the Baptist could not get a vote,
On account of his old fashioned, camel's-hair coat;
And the Penitent Thief, who died on the cross,
Was reminded that all his bones were broken!
Till at last, when each in turn had spoken,
The company being still at a loss,
The Angel, who had rolled away the stone,
Was sent to the sepulchre, all alone,
And filled with glory that gloomy prison,
And said to the Virgin, "The Lord is arisen!"

(The Cathedral bells ring.)

But hark! the bells are beginning to chime;
And I feel that I am growing hoarse.
I will put an end to my discourse,
And leave the rest for some other time.
For the bells themselves are the best of preachers;
Their brazen lips are learned teachers,
From their pulpits of stone, in the upper air,
Sounding aloft, without crack or flaw,
Shriller than trumpets under the Law,
Now a sermon and now a prayer.
The clangorous hammer is the tongue,
This way, that way, beaten and swung,
That from mouth of brass, as from Mouth of Gold,
May be taught the Testaments, New and Old.
And above it the great crossbeam of wood
Representeth the Holy Rood,

Upon which, like the bell, our hopes are hung.
And the wheel wherewith it is swayed and rung
Is the mind of man, that round and round
Sways, and maketh the tongue to sound!
And the rope, with its twisted cordage three,
Denoteth the Scriptural Trinity
Of Morals, and Symbols, and History;
And the upward and downward motions show
That we touch upon matters high and low;
And the constant change and transmutation
Of action and of contemplation,
Downward, the Scripture brought from on high,
Upward, exalted again to the sky;
Downward, the literal interpretation,
Upward, the Vision and Mystery!

And now, my hearers, to make an end,
I have only one word more to say;
In the church, in honor of Easter day,
Will be represented a Miracle Play;
And I hope you will all have the grace to attend.
Christ bring us at last So his felicity!
Pax vobiscum! et Benedicite!

IN THE CATHEDRAL.

CHAUNT.
> Kyrie Eleison!
> Christe Eleison!

Elsie. I am at home here in my Father's house!
These paintings of the Saints upon the walls

Have all familiar and benignant faces.

Prince Henry. The portraits of the family of God!
Thine own hereafter shall be placed among them.

Elsie. How very grand it is and wonderful!
Never have I beheld a church so splendid!
Such columns, and such arches, and such windows,
So many tombs and statues in the chapels,
And under them so many confessionals.
They must be for the rich. I should not like
To tell my sins in such a church as this.
Who built it?

Prince Henry. A great master of his craft,
Erwin von Steinbach; but not he alone,
For many generations labored with him.
Children that came to see these Saints in stone,
As day by day out of the blocks they rose,
Grew old and died, and still the work went on,
And on, and on, and is not yet completed.
The generation that succeeds our own
Perhaps may finish it. The architect
Built his great heart into these sculptured stones,
And with him toiled his children, and their lives
Were builded, with his own, into the walls,
As offerings unto God. You see that statue
Fixing its joyous, but deep-wrinkled eyes
Upon the Pillar of the Angels yonder.
That is the image of the master, carved
By the fair hand of his own child, Sabina.

The Golden Legend

Elsie. How beautiful is the column that he looks at!

Prince Henry. That, too, she sculptured. At the base of it
Stand the Evangelists; above their heads
Four Angels blowing upon marble trumpets,
And over them the blessed Christ, surrounded
By his attendant ministers, upholding
The instruments of his passion.

Elsie. O my Lord!
Would I could leave behind me upon earth
Some monument to thy glory, such as this!

Prince Henry. A greater monument than this thou leavest
In thine own life, all purity and love!
See, too, the Rose, above the western portal
Flamboyant with a thousand gorgeous colors,
The perfect flower of Gothic loveliness!

Elsie. And, in the gallery, the long line of statues,
Christ with his twelve Apostles watching us.

(A BISHOP *in armor, booted and spurred, passes with his train.*)

Prince Henry. But come away; we have not time to look.
The crowd already fills the church, and yonder
Upon a stage, a herald with a trumpet,
Clad like The Angel Gabriel, proclaims
The Mystery that will now be represented.

THE NATIVITY.
A MIRACLE PLAY.
THE NATIVITY.

INTROITUS.

Praeco. Come, good people, all and each,
Come and listen to our speech!
In your presence here I stand,
With a trumpet in my hand,
To announce the Easter Play,
Which we represent to-day!
First of all we shall rehearse,
In our action and our verse,
The Nativity of our Lord,
As written in the old record
Of the Protevangelion,
So that he who reads may run!

(Blows his trumpet.)

I. HEAVEN.

Mercy (at the feet of God). Have pity, Lord be not afraid
To save mankind, whom thou hast made,
Nor let the souls that were betrayed
  Perish eternally!

Justice. It cannot be, it must not be!
When in the garden placed by thee,
The fruit of the forbidden tree
  He ate, and he must die!

Mercy. Have pity, Lord! let penitence
Atone for disobedience,
Nor let the fruit of man's offence
  Be endless misery!

Justice. What penitence proportionate
Can e'er be felt for sin so great?
Of the forbidden fruit he ate,
  And damned must he be!

God. He shall be saved, if that within
The bounds of earth one free from sin
Be found, who for his kith and kin
  Will suffer martyrdom.

The Four Virtues. Lord! we have searched the world around,
From centre to the utmost bound,
But no such mortal can be found;
  Despairing, back we come.

Wisdom. No mortal, but a God made man,
Can ever carry out this plan,
Achieving what none other can,
  Salvation unto all!

God. Go, then, O my beloved Son;
It can by thee alone be done;
By thee the victory shall be won
  O'er Satan and the Fall!

(Here the ANGEL GABRIEL *shall leave Paradise and fly toward the earth; the jaws of Hell open below, and the Devils walk about, making a great noise.*)

II. MARY AT THE WELL.

Mary. Along the garden walk, and thence
Through the wicket in the garden fence,
  I steal with quiet pace,
My pitcher at the well to fill,
That lies so deep and cool and still
  In this sequestered place.
These sycamores keep guard around;
I see no face, I hear no sound,
  Save babblings of the spring,
And my companions, who within
The threads of gold and scarlet spin,
  And at their labor sing.

The Angel Gabriel. Hail, Virgin Mary, full of grace!

(Here MARY *looketh around her, trembling, and then saith:*)

Mary. Who is it speaketh in this place,
With such a gentle voice?

Gabriel. The Lord of heaven is with thee now!
Blessed among all women thou,
  Who art his holy choice!

Mary (setting down the pitcher). What can this mean?
No one is near,
And yet, such sacred words I hear,
  I almost fear to stay.

The Golden Legend

(Here the ANGEL, *appearing to her, shall say:*)

Gabriel. Fear not, O Mary! but believe!
For thou, a Virgin, shalt conceive
  A child this very day.

Fear not, O Mary! from the sky
The majesty of the Most High
  Shall overshadow thee!

Mary. Behold the handmaid of the Lord!
According to thy holy word,
  So be it unto me!

      (Here the Devils shall again make a great noise,
           under the stage.)

III. THE ANGELS OF THE SEVEN PLANETS,
    bearing the Star of Bethlehem.

The Angels. The Angels of the Planets Seven
Across the shining fields of heaven
  The natal star we bring!
Dropping our sevenfold virtues down,
As priceless jewels in the crown
  Of Christ, our new-born King.

Raphael. I am the Angel of the Sun,
Whose flaming wheels began to run
  When God's almighty breath
Said to the darkness and the Night,
Let there be light! and there was light!

I bring the gift of Faith.

Gabriel. I am the Angel of the Moon,
Darkened, to be rekindled soon
  Beneath the azure cope!
Nearest to earth, it is my ray
That best illumes the midnight way.
  I bring the gift of Hope!

Anael. The Angel of the Star of Love,
The Evening Star, that shines above
  The place where lovers be,
Above all happy hearths and homes,
On roofs of thatch, or golden domes,
  I give him Charity!

Zobiachel. The Planet Jupiter is mine!
The mightiest star of all that shine,
  Except the sun alone!
He is the High Priest of the Dove,
And sends, from his great throne above,
  Justice, that shall atone!

Michael. The Planet Mercury, whose place
Is nearest to the sun in space,
  Is my allotted sphere!
And with celestial ardor swift
I bear upon my hands the gift
  Of heavenly Prudence here!

Uriel. I am the Minister of Mars,
The strongest star among the stars!
  My songs of power prelude

The march and battle of man's life,
And for the suffering and the strife,
  I give him Fortitude!

Anachiel. The Angel of the uttermost
Of all the shining, heavenly host,
  From the far-off expanse
Of the Saturnian, endless space
I bring the last, the crowning grace,
  The gift of Temperance!

        (A sudden light shines from the windows of the stable
               in the village below.)

IV. THE WISE MEN OF THE EAST.

The stable of the Inn. The VIRGIN *and* CHILD.
Three Gypsy Kings, GASPAR, MELCHIOR, *and* BELSHAZZAR,
shall come in.

Gaspar. Hail to thee, Jesus of Nazareth!
Though in a manger thou drawest thy breath,
Thou art greater than Life and Death,
  Greater than Joy or Woe!
This cross upon the line of life
Portendeth struggle, toil, and strife,
And through a region with dangers rife
  In darkness shalt thou go!

Melchior. Hail to thee, King of Jerusalem
Though humbly born in Bethlehem,
A sceptre and a diadem

   Await thy brow and hand!
The sceptre is a simple reed,
The crown will make thy temples bleed,
And in thy hour of greatest need,
  Abashed thy subjects stand!

Belshazzar. Hail to thee, Christ of Christendom!
O'er all the earth thy kingdom come!
From distant Trebizond to Rome
  Thy name shall men adore!
Peace and good-will among all men,
The Virgin has returned again,
Returned the old Saturnian reign
  And Golden Age once more.

The Child Christ. Jesus, the Son of God, am I,
Born here to suffer and to die
According to the prophecy,
  That other men may live!

The Virgin. And now these clothes, that wrapped him, take
And keep them precious, for his sake;
For benediction thus we make,
  Naught else have we to give.

    (She gives them swaddling-clothes and they depart.)

V. THE FLIGHT INTO EGYPT.

Here shall JOSEPH *come in, leading an ass, on which are seated* MARY *and the* CHILD.

Mary. Here will we rest us, under these
Underhanging branches of the trees,
Where robins chant their Litanies,
   And canticles of joy.

Joseph. My saddle-girths have given way
With trudging through the heat to-day
To you I think it is but play
   To ride and hold the boy.

Mary. Hark! how the robins shout and sing,
As if to hail their infant King!
I will alight at yonder spring
   To wash his little coat.

Joseph. And I will hobble well the ass,
Lest, being loose upon the grass,
He should escape; for, by the mass.
   He is nimble as a goat.

   (Here MARY *shall alight and go to the spring.*)

Mary. O Joseph! I am much afraid,
For men are sleeping in the shade;
I fear that we shall be waylaid,
   And robbed and beaten sore!

(Here a band of robbers shall be seen sleeping, two of
whom shall rise and come forward.)

Dumachus. Cock's soul! deliver up your gold!

Joseph. I pray you, Sirs, let go your hold!
Of wealth I have no store.

Dumachus. Give up your money!

Titus. Prithee cease!
Let these good people go in peace!

Dumachus. First let them pay for their release,
And then go on their way.

Titus. These forty groats I give in fee,
If thou wilt only silent be.

Mary. May God be merciful to thee
Upon the Judgment Day!

Jesus. When thirty years shall have gone by,
I at Jerusalem shall die,
By Jewish hands exalted high
  On the accursed tree.
Then on my right and my left side,
These thieves shall both be crucified
And Titus thenceforth shall abide
  In paradise with me.

(Here a great rumor of trumpets and horses, like the

noise of a king with his army, and the robbers shall take flight.)

VI. THE SLAUGHTER OF THE INNOCENTS.

King Herod. Potz-tausend! Himmel-sacrament!
Filled am I with great wonderment
  At this unwelcome news!
Am I not Herod? Who shall dare
My crown to take, my sceptre bear,
  As king among the Jews?

    (Here he shall stride up and down and flourish his sword.)

What ho! I fain would drink a can
Of the strong wine of Canaan!
  The wine of Helbon bring,
I purchased at the Fair of Tyre,
As red as blood, as hot as fire,
  And fit for any king!

    (He quaffs great goblets of wine.)

Now at the window will I stand,
While in the street the armed band
  The little children slay:
The babe just born in Bethlehem
Will surely slaughtered be with them,
  Nor live another day!

    (Here a voice of lamentation shall be heard in the street.)

Rachel. O wicked king! O cruel speed!
To do this most unrighteous deed!
  My children all are slain!

Herod. Ho seneschal! another cup!
With wine of Sorek fill it up!
  I would a bumper drain!

Rahab. May maledictions fall and blast
Thyself and lineage, to the last
  Of all thy kith and kin!

Herod. Another goblet! quick! and stir
Pomegranate juice and drops of myrrh
  And calamus therein!

  Soldiers (in the street). Give up thy child into our hands!
It is King Herod who commands
  That he should thus be slain!

The Nurse Medusa. O monstrous men! What have ye done!
It is King Herod's only son
  That ye have cleft in twain!

Herod. Ah, luckless day! What words of fear
Are these that smite upon my ear
  With such a doleful sound!
What torments rack my heart and head!
Would I were dead! would I were dead,
  And buried in the ground!

    (He falls down and writhes as though eaten by worms.
    Hell opens, and SATAN *and* ASTAROTH *come forth,*

and drag him down.)

VII. JESUS AT PLAY WITH HIS SCHOOLMATES.

Jesus. The shower is over. Let us play,
And make some sparrows out of clay,
  Down by the river's side.

Judas. See, how the stream has overflowed
Its banks, and o'er the meadow road
  Is spreading far and wide!

> (They draw water out of the river by channels, and
> form little pools JESUS *makes twelve sparrows of
> clay, and the other boys do the same.*)

Jesus. Look! look! how prettily I make
These little sparrows by the lake
  Bend down their necks and drink!
Now will I make them sing and soar
So far, they shall return no more
  Into this river's brink.

Judas. That canst thou not! They are but clay,
They cannot sing, nor fly away
  Above the meadow lands!

Jesus. Fly, fly! ye sparrows! you are free!
And while you live, remember me,
  Who made you with my hands.

(Here JESUS *shall clap his hands, and the sparrows shall fly away, chirruping.*)

Judas. Thou art a sorcerer, I know;
Oft has my mother told me so,
  I will not play with thee!

(He strikes JESUS *on the right side.*)

Jesus. Ah, Judas! thou has smote my side,
And when I shall be crucified,
  There shall I pierced be!

(Here JOSEPH *shall come in, and say:*)

Joseph. Ye wicked boys! why do ye play,
And break the holy Sabbath day?
What, think ye, will your mothers say
  To see you in such plight!
In such a sweat and such a heat,
With all that mud-upon your feet!
There's not a beggar in the street
  Makes such a sorry sight!

VIII. THE VILLAGE SCHOOL.

The RABBI BEN ISRAEL, *with a long beard, sitting on a high stool, with a rod in his hand.*

Rabbi. I am the Rabbi Ben Israel,
Throughout this village known full well,
And, as my scholars all will tell,

Learned in things divine;
The Kabala and Talmud hoar
Than all the prophets prize I more,
For water is all Bible lore,
  But Mishna is strong wine.

My fame extends from West to East,
And always, at the Purim feast,
I am as drunk as any beast
  That wallows in his sty;
The wine it so elateth me,
That I no difference can see
Between "Accursed Haman be!"
  And "Blessed be Mordecai!"

Come hither, Judas Iscariot.
Say, if thy lesson thou hast got
From the Rabbinical Book or not.
  Why howl the dogs at night?

Judas. In the Rabbinical Book, it saith
The dogs howl, when with icy breath
Great Sammael, the Angel of Death,
  Takes through the town his flight!

Rabbi. Well, boy! now say, if thou art wise,
When the Angel of Death, who is full of eyes,
Comes where a sick man dying lies,
  What doth he to the wight?

Judas. He stands beside him, dark and tall,
Holding a sword, from which doth fall
Into his mouth a drop of gall,

And so he turneth white.

Rabbi. And now, my Judas, say to me
What the great Voices Four may be,
That quite across the world do flee,
  And are not heard by men?

Judas. The Voice of the Sun in heaven's dome,
The Voice of the Murmuring of Rome,
The Voice of a Soul that goeth home,
  And the Angel of the Rain!

Rabbi. Well have ye answered every one
Now little Jesus, the carpenter's son,
Let us see how thy task is done.
  Canst thou thy letters say?

Jesus. Aleph.

Rabbi. What next? Do not stop yet!
Go on with all the alphabet.
Come, Aleph, Beth; dost thou forget?
  Cock's soul! thou'dst rather play!

Jesus. What Aleph means I fain would know,
Before I any farther go!

Rabbi. O, by Saint Peter! wouldst thou so?
Come hither, boy, to me.
And surely as the letter Jod
Once cried aloud, and spake to God,
So surely shalt thou feel this rod,
  And punished shalt thou be!

The Golden Legend

(Here RABBI BEN ISRAEL *shall lift up his rod to strike*
JESUS, *and his right arm shall be paralyzed.*)

IX. CROWNED WITH FLOWERS.

JESUS *sitting among his playmates, crowned with flowers as their King.*

Boys. We spread our garments on the ground'
With fragrant flowers thy head is crowned,
While like a guard we stand around,
  And hail thee as our King!
Thou art the new King of the Jews!
Nor let the passers-by refuse
To bring that homage which men use
  To majesty to bring.

    (Here a traveller shall go by, and the boys shall lay
      hold of his garments and say:)

Boys. Come hither! and all reverence pay
Unto our monarch, crowned to-day!
Then go rejoicing on your way,
  In all prosperity!

Traveller. Hail to the King of Bethlehem,
Who weareth in his diadem
The yellow crocus for the gem
  Of his authority!

    (He passes by; and others come in, bearing on a litter

a sick child.)

Boys. Set down the litter and draw near!
The King of Bethlehem is here!
What ails the child, who seems to fear
  That we shall do him harm?

The Bearers. He climbed up to the robin's nest,
And out there darted, from his rest,
A serpent with a crimson crest,
  And stung him in the arm.

Jesus. Bring him to me, and let me feel
The wounded place; my touch can heal
The sting of serpents, and can steal
  The poison from the bite!

    (He touches the wound, and the boy begins to cry.)

Cease to lament! I can foresee
That thou hereafter known shalt be,
Among the men who follow me,
  As Simon the Canaanite!

EPILOGUE.

In the after part of the day
Will be represented another play,
Of the Passion of our Blessed Lord,
Beginning directly after Nones!
At the close of which we shall accord,
By way of benison and reward,
The sight of a holy Martyr's bones!

IV. THE ROAD HIRSCHAU.

PRINCE HENRY *and* ELSIE, *with their attendants, on horseback.*

Elsie. Onward and onward the highway runs
    to the distant city, impatiently bearing
Tidings of human joy and disaster, of love and of
    hate, of doing and daring!

Prince Henry. This life of ours is a wild aeolian
    harp of many a joyous strain,
But under them all there runs a loud perpetual wail,

as of souls in pain.

Elsie. Faith alone can interpret life, and the heart that aches and bleeds with the stigma
Of pain, alone bears the likeness of Christ, and can comprehend its dark enigma.

Prince Henry. Man is selfish, and seeketh pleasure with little care of what may betide;
Else why am I travelling here beside thee, a demon that rides by an angel's side?

Elsie. All the hedges are white with dust, and the great dog under the creaking wain
Hangs his head in the lazy heat, while onward the horses toil and strain

Prince Henry. Now they stop at the wayside inn, and the wagoner laughs with the landlord's daughter,
While out of the dripping trough the horses distend their leathern sides with water.

Elsie. All through life there are wayside inns, where man may refresh his soul with love;
Even the lowest may quench his thirst at rivulets fed by springs from above.

Prince Henry. Yonder, where rises the cross of stone, our journey along the highway ends,
And over the fields, by a bridle path, down into the broad green valley descends.

Elsie. I am not sorry to leave behind the beaten

road with its dust and heat;
The air will be sweeter far, and the turf will be softer
 under our horses' feet.

(They turn down a green lane.)

Elsie. Sweet is the air with the budding haws,
 and the valley stretching for miles below
Is white with blossoming cheery trees, as if just covered
 with lightest snow.

Prince Henry. Over our heads a white cascade is
 gleaming against the distant hill;
We cannot hear it, nor see it move, but it hangs like
 a banner when winds are still.

Elsie. Damp and cool is this deep ravine, and
 cool the sound of the brook by our side!
What is this castle that rises above us, and lords it
 over a land so wide?

Prince Henry. It is the home of the Counts of
 Calva; well have I known these scenes of old,
Well I remember each tower and turret, remember the
 brooklet, the wood, and the wold.

Elsie. Hark! from the little village below us the
 bells of the church are ringing for rain!
Priests and peasants in long procession come forth
 and kneel on the arid plain.

Prince Henry. They have not long to wait, for I
 see in the south uprising a little cloud,

That before the sun shall be set will cover the sky
  above us as with a shroud.

    (*They pass on.*)

THE CONVENT OF HIRSCHAU IN THE
BLACK FOREST.

The Convent cellar. FRIAR CLAUS *comes in with a light and a basket of empty flagons.*

  Friar Claus. I always enter this sacred place
With a thoughtful, solemn, and reverent pace,
Pausing long enough on each stair
To breathe an ejaculatory prayer,
And a benediction on the vines
That produce these various sorts of wines!

For my part, I am well content
That we have got through with the tedious Lent!
Fasting is all very well for those
Who have to contend with invisible foes;
But I am quite sure it does not agree
With a quiet, peaceable man like me,
Who am not of that nervous and meagre kind
That are always distressed in body and mind!
And at times it really does me good
To come down among this brotherhood,
Dwelling forever under ground,
Silent, contemplative, round and sound;
Each one old, and brown with mould,
But filled to the lips with the ardor of youth,
With the latent power and love of truth,

And with virtues fervent and manifold.
I have heard it said, that at Easter-tide,
When buds are swelling on every side,
And the sap begins to move in the vine.
Then in all the cellars, far and wide,
The oldest, as well as the newest, wine
Begins to stir itself, and ferment,
With a kind of revolt and discontent
At being so long in darkness pent,
And fain would burst from its sombre tun
To bask on the hillside in the sun;
As in the bosom of us poor friars,
The tumult of half-subdued desires
For the world that we have left behind
Disturbs at times all peace of mind!
And now that we have lived through Lent,
My duty it is, as often before,
To open awhile the prison-door,
And give these restless spirits vent.

Now here is a cask that stands alone,
And has stood a hundred years or more,
Its beard of cobwebs, long and hoar,
Trailing and sweeping along the floor,
Like Barbarossa, who sits in his cave,
Taciturn, sombre, sedate, and grave,
Till his beard has grown through the table of stone!
It is of the quick and not of the dead!
In its veins the blood is hot and red,
And a heart still beats in those ribs of oak
That time may have tamed, but has not broke;
It comes from Bacharach on the Rhine,
Is one of the three best kinds of wine,

And costs some hundred florins the ohm;
But that I do not consider dear,
When I remember that every year
Four butts are sent to the Pope of Rome.
And whenever a goblet thereof I drain,
The old rhyme keeps running in my brain:

    At Bacharach on the Rhine,
    At Hochheim on the Main,
    And at Wuerzburg on the Stein,
    Grow the three best kinds of wine!

They are all good wines, and better far
Than those of the Neckar, or those of the Ahr
In particular, Wuerzburg well may boast
Of its blessed wine of the Holy Ghost,
Which of all wines I like the most.
This I shall draw for the Abbot's drinking,
Who seems to be much of my way of thinking.

    (Fills a flagon.)

Ah! how the streamlet laughs and sings!
What a delicious fragrance springs
From the deep flagon, while it fills,
As of hyacinths and daffodils!
Between this cask and the Abbot's lips
Many have been the sips and slips;
Many have been the draughts of wine,
On their way to his, that have stopped at mine;
And many a time my soul has hankered
For a deep draught out of his silver tankard,
When it should have been busy with other affairs,

Less with its longings and more with its prayers.
But now there is no such awkward condition,
No danger of death and eternal perdition;
So here's to the Abbot and Brothers all,
Who dwell in this convent of Peter and Paul!

    (He drinks.)

O cordial delicious! O soother of pain!
It flashes like sunshine into my brain!
A benison rest on the Bishop who sends
Such a fudder of wine as this to his friends!

And now a flagon for such as may ask
A draught from the noble Bacharach cask,
And I will be gone, though I know full well
The cellar's a cheerfuller place than the cell.
Behold where he stands, all sound and good,
Brown and old in his oaken hood;
Silent he seems externally
As any Carthusian monk may be;
But within, what a spirit of deep unrest!
What a seething and simmering in his breast!
As if the heaving of his great heart
Would burst his belt of oak apart!
Let me unloose this button of wood,
And quiet a little his turbulent mood.

    (Sets it running.)

See! how its currents gleam and shine,
As if they had caught the purple hues
Of autumn sunsets on the Rhine,

Descending and mingling with the dews;
Or as if the grapes were stained with the blood
Of the innocent boy, who, some years back,
Was taken and crucified by the Jews,
In that ancient town of Bacharach;
Perdition upon those infidel Jews,
In that ancient town of Bacharach!
The beautiful town, that gives us wine
With the fragrant odor of Muscadine!
I should deem it wrong to let this pass
Without first touching my lips to the glass,
For here in the midst of the current I stand,
Like the stone Pfalz in the midst of the river
Taking toll upon either hand,
And much more grateful to the giver.

    (He drinks.)

Here, now, is a very inferior kind,
Such as in any town you may find,
Such as one might imagine would suit
The rascal who drank wine out of a boot,
And, after all, it was not a crime,
For he won thereby Dorf Hueffelsheim.
A jolly old toper! who at a pull
Could drink a postilion's jack boot full,
And ask with a laugh, when that was done,
If the fellow had left the other one!
This wine is as good as we can afford
To the friars, who sit at the lower board,
And cannot distinguish bad from good,
And are far better off than if they could,
Being rather the rude disciples of beer

Than of anything more refined and dear!

(Fills the other flagon and departs.)

THE SCRIPTORIUM.

FRIAR PACIFICUS *transcribing and illuminating.*

Friar Pacificus It is growing dark! Yet one line more,
And then my work for today is o'er.
I come again to the name of the Lord!
Ere I that awful name record,
That is spoken so lightly among men,
Let me pause awhile, and wash my pen;
Pure from blemish and blot must it be
When it writes that word of mystery!

Thus have I labored on and on,
Nearly through the Gospel of John.
Can it be that from the lips
Of this same gentle Evangelist,
That Christ himself perhaps has kissed,
Came the dread Apocalypse!
It has a very awful look,
As it stands there at the end of the book,
Like the sun in an eclipse.
Ah me! when I think of that vision divine,
Think of writing it, line by line,
I stand in awe of the terrible curse,
Like the trump of doom, in the closing verse!
God forgive me! if ever I
Take aught from the book of that Prophecy,
Lest my part too should be taken away

From the Book of Life on the Judgment Day.

This is well written, though I say it!
I should not be afraid to display it,
In open day, on the selfsame shelf
With the writings of St Thecla herself,
Or of Theodosius, who of old
Wrote the Gospels in letters of gold!
That goodly folio standing yonder,
Without a single blot or blunder,
Would not bear away the palm from mine,
If we should compare them line for line.

There, now, is an initial letter!
King Rene himself never made a better!
Finished down to the leaf and the snail,
Down to the eyes on the peacock's tail!
And now, as I turn the volume over,
And see what lies between cover and cover,
What treasures of art these pages hold,
All ablaze with crimson and gold,
God forgive me! I seem to feel
A certain satisfaction steal
Into my heart, and into my brain,
As if my talent had not lain
Wrapped in a napkin, and all in vain.
Yes, I might almost say to the Lord,
Here is a copy of thy Word,
Written out with much toil and pain;
Take it, O Lord, and let it be
As something I have done for thee!

(He looks from the window.)

How sweet the air is! How fair the scene!
I wish I had as lovely a green
To paint my landscapes and my leaves!
How the swallows twitter under the eaves!
There, now, there is one in her nest;
I can just catch a glimpse of her head and breast,
And will sketch her thus, in her quiet nook,
In the margin of my Gospel book.

(He makes a sketch.)

I can see no more. Through the valley yonder
A shower is passing; I hear the thunder
Mutter its curses in the air,
The Devil's own and only prayer!
The dusty road is brown with rain,
And speeding on with might and main,
Hitherward rides a gallant train.
They do not parley, they cannot wait,
But hurry in at the convent gate.
What a fair lady! and beside her
What a handsome, graceful, noble rider!
Now she gives him her hand to alight;
They will beg a shelter for the night.
I will go down to the corridor,
And try to see that face once more;
It will do for the face of some beautiful Saint,
Or for one of the Maries I shall paint.

(Goes out.)

THE CLOISTERS.

The ABBOT ERNESTUS *pacing to and fro.*

  Abbot. Slowly, slowly up the wall
Steals the sunshine, steals the shade;
Evening damps begin to fall,
Evening shadows are displayed.
Round me, o'er me, everywhere,
All the sky is grand with clouds,
And athwart the evening air
Wheel the swallows home in crowds.
Shafts of sunshine from the west
Paint the dusky windows red;
Darker shadows, deeper rest,
Underneath and overhead.
Darker, darker, and more wan,
In my breast the shadows fall;
Upward steals the life of man,
As the sunshine from the wall.
From the wall into the sky,
From the roof along the spire;
Ah, the souls of those that die
Are but sunbeams lifted higher.

      (Enter PRINCE HENRY.)

  Prince Henry. Christ is arisen!

  Abbot. Amen! he is arisen!
His peace be with you!

The Golden Legend

Prince Henry. Here it reigns forever!
The peace of God, that passeth understanding,
Reigns in these cloisters and these corridors,
Are you Ernestus, Abbot of the convent?

Abbot. I am.

Prince Henry. And I Prince Henry of Hoheneck,
Who crave your hospitality to-night.

Abbot. You are thrice welcome to our humble walls.
You do us honor; and we shall requite it,
I fear, but poorly, entertaining you
With Paschal eggs, and our poor convent wine,
The remnants of our Easter holidays.

Prince Henry. How fares it with the holy monks of Hirschau?
Are all things well with them?

Abbot. All things are well.

Prince Henry. A noble convent! I have known it long
By the report of travellers. I now see
Their commendations lag behind the truth.
You lie here in the valley of the Nagold
As in a nest: and the still river, gliding
Along its bed, is like an admonition
How all things pass. Your lands are rich and ample,
And your revenues large. God's benediction
Rests on your convent.

Abbot. By our charities
We strive to merit it. Our Lord and Master,

When he departed, left us in his will,
As our best legacy on earth, the poor!
These we have always with us; had we not,
Our hearts would grow as hard as are these stones.

Prince Henry. If I remember right, the Counts of Calva
Founded your convent.

Abbot. Even as you say.

Prince Henry. And, if I err not, it is very old.

Abbot. Within these cloisters lie already buried
Twelve holy Abbots. Underneath the flags
On which we stand, the Abbot William lies,
Of blessed memory.

Prince Henry. And whose tomb is that,
Which bears the brass escutcheon?

Abbot. A benefactor's.
Conrad, a Count of Calva, he who stood
Godfather to our bells.

Prince Henry. Your monks are learned
And holy men, I trust.

Abbot. There are among them
Learned and holy men. Yet in this age
We need another Hildebrand, to shake
And purify us like a mighty wind.
The world is wicked, and sometimes I wonder
God does not lose his patience with it wholly,

And shatter it like glass! Even here, at times,
Within these walls, where all should be at peace,
I have my trials. Time has laid his hand
Upon my heart, gently, not smiting it,
But as a harper lays his open palm
Upon his harp, to deaden its vibrations.
Ashes are on my head, and on my lips
Sackcloth, and in my breast a heaviness
And weariness of life, that makes me ready
To say to the dead Abbots under us,
"Make room for me!" Only I see the dusk
Of evening twilight coming, and have not
Completed half my task; and so at times
The thought of my shortcomings in this life
Falls like a shadow on the life to come.

Prince Henry. We must all die, and not the old alone;
The young have no exemption from that doom.

Abbot. Ah, yes! the young may die, but the old must!
That is the difference.

Prince Henry. I have heard much laud
Of your transcribers. Your Scriptorium
Is famous among all, your manuscripts
Praised for their beauty and their excellence.

Abbot. That is indeed our boast. If you desire it,
You shall behold these treasures. And meanwhile
Shall the Refectorarius bestow
Your horses and attendants for the night.

(They go in. The Vesper-bell rings.)

THE CHAPEL.

Vespers; after which the monks retire, a chorister
leading an old monk who is blind.

  Prince Henry. They are all gone, save one who lingers,
Absorbed in deep and silent prayer.
As if his heart could find no rest,
At times he beats his heaving breast
With clenched and convulsive fingers,
Then lifts them trembling in the air.
A chorister, with golden hair,
Guides hitherward his heavy pace.
Can it be so? Or does my sight
Deceive me in the uncertain light?
Ah no! I recognize that face,
Though Time has touched it in his flight,
And changed the auburn hair to white.
It is Count Hugo of the Rhine,
The deadliest foe of all our race,
And hateful unto me and mine!

  The Blind Monk. Who is it that doth stand so near
His whispered words I almost hear?

  Prince Henry. I am Prince Henry of Hoheneck,
And you, Count Hugo of the Rhine!
I know you, and I see the scar,
The brand upon your forehead, shine
And redden like a baleful star!

  The Blind Monk. Count Hugo once, but now the wreck

The Golden Legend

Of what I was. O Hoheneck!
The passionate will, the pride, the wrath
That bore me headlong on my path,
Stumbled and staggered into fear,
And failed me in my mad career,
As a tired steed some evil-doer,
Alone upon a desolate moor,
Bewildered, lost, deserted, blind,
And hearing loud and close behind
The o'ertaking steps of his pursuer.
Then suddenly, from the dark there came
A voice that called me by my name,
And said to me, "Kneel down and pray!"
And so my terror passed away,
Passed utterly away forever.
Contrition, penitence, remorse,
Came on me, with o'erwhelming force;
A hope, a longing, an endeavor,
By days of penance and nights of prayer,
To frustrate and defeat despair!
Calm, deep, and still is now my heart.
With tranquil waters overflowed;
A lake whose unseen fountains start,
Where once the hot volcano glowed.
And you, O Prince of Hoheneck!
Have known me in that earlier time,
A man of violence and crime,
Whose passions brooked no curb nor check.
Behold me now, in gentler mood,
One of this holy brotherhood.
Give me your hand; here let me kneel;
Make your reproaches sharp as steel;
Spurn me, and smite me on each cheek;

No violence can harm the meek,
There is no wound Christ cannot heal!
Yes; lift your princely hand, and take
Revenge, if 't is revenge you seek,
Then pardon me, for Jesus' sake!

Prince Henry. Arise, Count Hugo! let there be
No farther strife nor enmity
Between us twain; we both have erred!
Too rash in act, too wroth in word,
From the beginning have we stood
In fierce, defiant attitude,
Each thoughtless of the other's right,
And each reliant on his might.
But now our souls are more subdued;
The hand of God, and not in vain,
Has touched us with the fire of pain.
Let us kneel down, and side by side
Pray, till our souls are purified,
And pardon will not be denied!

(They kneel.)

THE REFECTORY.

Gaudiolum of Monks at midnight. LUCIFER disguised as a Friar.

Friar Paul (sings). Ave! color vini clari,
    Dulcis potus, non aman,
    Tua nos inebriari
      Digneris potentia!

Friar Cuthbert. Not so much noise, my worthy freres,
You'll disturb the Abbot at his prayers.
   Friar Paul (sings). O! quam placens in colore!
      O! quam fragrans in odore!
      O! quam sapidum in ore!
        Dulce linguse vinculum!

Friar Cuthbert. I should think your tongue had
broken its chain!

   Friar Paul (sings). Felix venter quern intrabis!
      Felix guttur quod rigabis!
      Felix os quod tu lavabis!
        Et beata labia!

Friar Cuthbert. Peace! I say, peace!
Will you never cease!
You will rouse up the Abbot, I tell you again!

Friar John. No danger! to-night he will let us alone,
As I happen to know he has guests of his own.

Friar Cuthbert. Who are they?

Friar John. A German Prince and his train,
Who arrived here just before the rain.
There is with him a damsel fair to see,
As slender and graceful as a reed!
When she alighted from her steed,
It seemed like a blossom blown from a tree.

Friar Cuthbert. None of your pale-faced girls for me!

(Kisses the girl at his side.)

Friar John. Come, old fellow, drink down to your peg!
do not drink any farther, I beg!

Friar Paul (sings). In the days of gold,
    The days of old,
    Cross of wood
    And bishop of gold!

Friar Cuthbert (to the girl). What an infernal racket and din!
No need not blush so, that's no sin.
You look very holy in this disguise,
Though there's something wicked in your eyes!

Friar Paul (continues.) Now we have changed
    That law so good,
    To cross of gold
    And bishop of wood!

Friar Cuthbert. I like your sweet face under a hood.
Sister! how came you into this way?

Girl. It was you, Friar Cuthbert, who led me astray.
Have you forgotten that day in June,
When the church was so cool in the afternoon,
And I came in to confess my sins?
That is where my ruin begins.

Friar John. What is the name of yonder friar,
With an eye that glows like a coal of fire,
And such a black mass of tangled hair?

Friar Paul. He who is sitting there,
With a rollicking,
Devil may care,
Free and easy look and air,
As if he were used to such feasting and frollicking?

Friar John. The same.

Friar Paul. He's a stranger. You had better ask his name,
And where he is going, and whence he came.

Friar John. Hallo! Sir Friar!

Friar Paul. You must raise your voice a little higher,
He does not seem to hear what you say.
Now, try again! He is looking this way.

Friar John. Hallo! Sir Friar,
We wish to inquire
Whence you came, and where you are going,
And anything else that is worth the knowing.
So be so good as to open your head.

Lucifer. I am a Frenchman born and bred,
Going on a pilgrimage to Rome.
My home
Is the convent of St. Gildas de Rhuys,
Of which, very like, you never have heard.

Monks. Never a word!

Lucifer. You must know, then, it is in the diocese
Called the Diocese of Vannes,

In the province of Brittany.
From the gray rocks of Morbihan
It overlooks the angry sea;
The very seashore where,
In his great despair,
Abbot Abelard walked to and fro,
Filling the night with woe,
And wailing aloud to the merciless seas
The name of his sweet Heloise!
Whilst overhead
The convent windows gleamed as red
As the fiery eyes of the monks within,
Who with jovial din
Gave themselves up to all kinds of sin!
Ha! that is a convent! that is an abbey!
Over the doors,
None of your death-heads carved in wood,
None of your Saints looking pious and good,
None of your Patriarchs old and shabby!
But the heads and tusks of boars,
And the cells
Hung all round with the fells
of the fallow-deer,
And then what cheer!
What jolly, fat friars,
Sitting round the great, roaring fires,
Roaring louder than they,
With their strong wines,
And their concubines,
And never a bell,
With its swagger and swell,
Calling you up with a start of affright
In the dead of night,

To send you grumbling down dark stairs,
To mumble your prayers,
But the cheery crow
Of cocks in the yard below,
After daybreak, an hour or so,
And the barking of deep-mouthed hounds,
These are the sounds
That, instead of bells, salute the ear.
And then all day
Up and away
Through the forest, hunting the deer!
Ah, my friends! I'm afraid that here
You are a little too pious, a little too tame,
And the more is the shame,
It is the greatest folly
Not to be jolly;
That's what I think!
Come, drink, drink,
Drink, and die game!

Monks. And your Abbot What's-his-name?

Lucifer. Abelard!

Monks. Did he drink hard?

Lucifer. O, no! Not he!
He was a dry old fellow,
Without juice enough to get thoroughly mellow.
There he stood,
Lowering at us in sullen mood,
As if he had come into Brittany
Just to reform our brotherhood!

(A roar of laughter.)

But you see
It never would do!
For some of us knew a thing or two,
In the Abbey of St. Gildas de Rhuys!
For instance, the great ado
With old Fulbert's niece,
The young and lovely Heloise!

Friar John. Stop there, if you please,
Till we drink to the fair Heloise.

All (drinking and shouting). Heloise! Heloise!

(The Chapel-bell tolls.)

Lucifer (starting). What is that bell for? Are you such asses
As to keep up the fashion of midnight masses?

Friar Cuthbert. It is only a poor, unfortunate brother,
Who is gifted with most miraculous powers
Of getting up at all sorts of hours,
And, by way of penance and Christian meekness,
Of creeping silently out of his cell
To take a pull at that hideous bell;
So that all the monks who are lying awake
May murmur some kind of prayer for his sake,
And adapted to his peculiar weakness!

Friar John. From frailty and fall--

All. Good Lord, deliver us all!

Friar Cuthbert. And before the bell for matins sounds,
He takes his lantern, and goes the rounds,
Flashing it into our sleepy eyes,
Merely to say it is time to arise.
But enough of that. Go on, if you please,
With your story about St. Gildas de Rhuys.

Lucifer. Well, it finally came to pass
That, half in fun and half in malice,
One Sunday at Mass
We put some poison into the chalice.
But, either by accident or design,
Peter Abelard kept away
From the chapel that day,
And a poor, young friar, who in his stead
Drank the sacramental wine,
Fell on the steps of the altar, dead!
But look! do you see at the window there
That face, with a look of grief and despair,
That ghastly face, as of one in pain?

Monks. Who? where?

Lucifer. As I spoke, it vanished away again.

Friar Cuthbert. It is that nefarious
Siebald the Refectorarius.
That fellow is always playing the scout,
Creeping and peeping and prowling about;
And then he regales
The Abbot with Scandalous tales.

Lucifer. A spy in the convent? One of the brothers

Telling scandalous tales of the others?
Out upon him, the lazy loon!
I would put a stop to that pretty soon,
In a way he should rue it.

Monks. How shall we do it?

Lucifer. Do you, brother Paul,
Creep under the window, close to the wall,
And open it suddenly when I call.
Then seize the villain by the hair,
And hold him there,
And punish him soundly, once for all.

Friar Cuthbert. As St. Dustan of old,
We are told,
Once caught the Devil by the nose!

Lucifer. Ha! ha! that story is very clever,
But has no foundation whatsoever.
Quick! for I see his face again
Glaring in at the window pane;
Now! now! and do not spare your blows.

(FRIAR PAUL *opens the window suddenly, and seizes*
SIEBALD. *They beat him.*)

Friar Siebald. Help! help! are you going to slay me?

Friar Paul. That will teach you again to betray me!

Friar Siebald. Mercy! mercy!

The Golden Legend

Friar Paul (shouting and beating). Rumpas bellorum lorum,
    Vim confer amorum
    Morum verorum, rorun.
    Tu plena polorum!

Lucifer. Who stands in the doorway yonder,
Stretching out his trembling hand,
Just as Abelard used to stand,
The flash of his keen, black eyes
Forerunning the thunder?

  The Monks (in confusion). The Abbot! the Abbot!

  Friar Cuthbert (to the girl). Put on your disguise!

Friar Francis. Hide the great flagon
From the eyes of the dragon!

Friar Cuthbert. Pull the brown hood over your face,
Lest you bring me into disgrace!

Abbot. What means this revel and carouse?
Is this a tavern and drinking-house?
Are you Christian monks, or heathen devils,
To pollute this convent with your revels?
Were Peter Damian still upon earth,
To be shocked by such ungodly mirth,
He would write your names, with pen of gall,
In his Book of Gomorrah, one and all!
Away, you drunkards! to your cells,
And pray till you hear the matin-bells;
You, Brother Francis, and you, Brother Paul!

And as a penance mark each prayer
With the scourge upon your shoulders bare;
Nothing atones for such a sin
But the blood that follows the discipline.
And you, Brother Cuthbert, come with me
Alone into the sacristy;
You, who should be a guide to your brothers,
And are ten times worse than all the others,
For you I've a draught that has long been brewing
You shall do a penance worth the doing!
Away to your prayers, then, one and all!
I wonder the very, convent wall
Does not crumble and crush you in its fall!

THE NEIGHBORING NUNNERY.

The ABBESS IRMINGARD *sitting with* ELSIE *in the moonlight.*

Irmingard The night is silent, the wind is still,
The moon is looking from yonder hill
Down upon convent, and grove, and garden;
The clouds have passed away from her face,
Leaving behind them no sorrowful trace,
Only the tender and quiet grace
Of one, whose heart had been healed with pardon!

And such am I. My soul within
Was dark with passion and soiled with sin.
But now its wounds are healed again;
Gone are the anguish, the terror, and pain;
For across that desolate land of woe,
O'er whose burning sands I was forced to go,

The Golden Legend

A wind from heaven began to blow;
And all my being trembled and shook,
As the leaves of the tree, or the grass of the field,
And I was healed, as the sick are healed,
When fanned by the leaves of the Holy Book!

As thou sittest in the moonlight there,
Its glory flooding thy golden hair,
And the only darkness that which lies
In the haunted chambers of thine eyes,
I feel my soul drawn unto thee,
Strangely, and strongly, and more and more,
As to one I have known and loved before;
For every soul is akin to me
That dwells in the land of mystery!
I am the Lady Irmingard,
Born of a noble race and name!
Many a wandering Suabian bard,
Whose life was dreary, and bleak, and hard,
Has found through me the way to fame.
Brief and bright were those days, and the night
Which followed was full of a lurid light.
Love, that of every woman's heart
Will have the whole, and not a part,
That is to her, in Nature's plan,
More than ambition is to man,
Her light, her life, her very breath,
With no alternative but death,
Found me a maiden soft and young,
Just from the convent's cloistered school,
And seated on my lowly stool,
Attentive while the minstrels sung.

Gallant, graceful, gentle, tall,
Fairest, noblest, best of all,
Was Walter of the Vogelweid,
And, whatsoever may betide,
Still I think of him with pride!
His song was of the summer-time
The very birds sang in his rhyme;
The sunshine, the delicious air,
The fragrance of the flowers, were there,
And I grew restless as I heard,
Restless and buoyant as a bird,
Down soft, aerial currents sailing,
O'er blossomed orchards, and fields in bloom,
And through the momentary gloom
Of shadows o'er the landscape trailing,
Yielding and borne I knew not where,
But feeling resistance unavailing.

And thus, unnoticed and apart,
And more by accident than choice.
I listened to that single voice
Until the chambers of my heart
Were filled with it by night and day,
One night,--it was a night in May,--
Within the garden, unawares,
Under the blossoms in the gloom,
I heard it utter my own name
With protestations and wild prayers;
And it rang through me, and became
Like the archangel's trump of doom,
Which the soul hears, and must obey;
And mine arose as from a tomb.
My former life now seemed to me

Such as hereafter death may be,
When in the great Eternity
We shall awake and find it day.

It was a dream, and would not stay;
A dream, that in a single night
Faded and vanished out of sight.
My father's anger followed fast
This passion, as a freshening blast
Seeks out and fans the fire, whose rage
It may increase, but not assuage.
And he exclaimed: "No wandering bard
Shall win thy hand, O Irmingard!
For which Prince Henry of Hoheneck
By messenger and letter sues."

Gently, but firmly, I replied:
"Henry of Hoheneck I discard!
Never the hand of Irmingard
Shall lie in his as the hand of a bride!"
This said I, Walter, for thy sake:
This said I, for I could not choose.
After a pause, my father spake
In that cold and deliberate tone
Which turns the hearer into stone,
And seems itself the act to be
That follows with such dread certainty;
"This, or the cloister and the veil!"
No other words than these he said,
But they were like a funeral wail;
My life was ended, my heart was dead.

That night from the castle-gate went down,

With silent, slow, and stealthy pace,
Two shadows, mounted on shadowy steeds,
Taking the narrow path that leads
Into the forest dense and brown,
In the leafy darkness of the place,
One could not distinguish form nor face,
Only a bulk without a shape,
A darker shadow in the shade;
One scarce could say it moved or stayed,
Thus it was we made our escape!
A foaming brook, with many a bound,
Followed us like a playful hound;
Then leaped before us, and in the hollow
Paused, and waited for us to follow,
And seemed impatient, and afraid
That our tardy flight should be betrayed
By the sound our horses' hoof-beats made,
And when we reached the plain below,
He paused a moment and drew rein
To look back at the castle again;
And we saw the windows all aglow
With lights, that were passing to and fro;
Our hearts with terror ceased to beat;
The brook crept silent to our feet;
We knew what most we feared to know.
Then suddenly horns began to blow;
And we heard a shout, and a heavy tramp,
And our horses snorted in the damp
Night-air of the meadows green and wide,
And in a moment, side by side,
So close, they must have seemed but one,
The shadows across the moonlight run,
And another came, and swept behind,

Like the shadow of clouds before the wind!

How I remember that breathless flight
Across the moors, in the summer night!
How under our feet the long, white road
Backward like a river flowed,
Sweeping with it fences and hedges,
Whilst farther away, and overhead,
Paler than I, with fear and dread,
The moon fled with us, as we fled
Along the forest's jagged edges!

All this I can remember well;
But of what afterward befell
I nothing farther can recall
Than a blind, desperate, headlong fall;
The rest is a blank and darkness all.
When I awoke out of this swoon,
The sun was shining, not the moon,
Making a cross upon the wall
With the bars of my windows narrow and tall;
And I prayed to it, as I had been wont to pray,
From early childhood, day by day,
Each morning, as in bed I lay!
I was lying again in my own room!
And I thanked God, in my fever and pain,
That those shadows on the midnight plain
Were gone, and could not come again!
I struggled no longer with my doom!
This happened many years ago.
I left my father's home to come
Like Catherine to her martyrdom,
For blindly I esteemed it so.

And when I heard the convent door
Behind me close, to ope no more,
I felt it smite me like a blow,
Through all my limbs a shudder ran,
And on my bruised spirit fell
The dampness of my narrow cell
As night-air on a wounded man,
Giving intolerable pain.

But now a better life began,
I felt the agony decrease
By slow degrees, then wholly cease,
Ending in perfect rest and peace!
It was not apathy, nor dulness,
That weighed and pressed upon my brain,
But the same passion I had given
To earth before, now turned to heaven
With all its overflowing fulness.

Alas! the world is full of peril!
The path that runs through the fairest meads,
On the sunniest side of the valley, leads
Into a region bleak and sterile!
Alike in the high-born and the lowly,
The will is feeble, and passion strong.
We cannot sever right from wrong;
Some falsehood mingles with all truth;
Nor is it strange the heart of youth
Should waver and comprehend but slowly
The things that are holy and unholy!

But in this sacred and calm retreat,
We are all well and safely shielded

From winds that blow, and waves that beat,
From the cold, and rain, and blighting heat,
To which the strongest hearts have yielded.
Here we stand as the Virgins Seven,
For our celestial bridegroom yearning;
Our hearts are lamps forever burning,
With a steady and unwavering flame,
Pointing upward, forever the same,
Steadily upward toward the Heaven!

The moon is hidden behind a cloud;
A sudden darkness fills the room,
And thy deep eyes, amid the gloom,
Shine like jewels in a shroud.
On the leaves is a sound of falling rain;
A bird, awakened in its nest,
Gives a faint twitter of unrest,
Then smoothes its plumes and sleeps again.

No other sounds than these I hear;
The hour of midnight must be near.
Thou art o'erspent with the day's fatigue
Of riding many a dusty league;
Sink, then, gently to thy slumber;
Me so many cares encumber,
So many ghosts, and forms of fright,
Have started from their graves to-night,
They have driven sleep from mine eyes away:
I will go down to the chapel and pray.

V. A COVERED BRIDGE AT LUCERNE.

Prince Henry. God's blessing on the architects who build
The bridges o'er swift rivers and abysses
Before impassable to human feet,
No less than on the builders of cathedrals,
Whose massive walls are bridges thrown across
The dark and terrible abyss of Death.
Well has the name of Pontifex been given
Unto the Church's head, as the chief builder
And architect of the invisible bridge
That leads from earth to heaven.

Elsie How dark it grows!
What are these paintings on the walls around us?

Prince Henry The Dance Macaber!

Elsie What?

Prince Henry The Dance of Death!
All that go to and fro must look upon it,
Mindful of what they shall be, while beneath,
Among the wooden piles, the turbulent river
Rushes, impetuous as the river of life,

The Golden Legend

With dimpling eddies, ever green and bright,
Save where the shadow of this bridge falls on it.

Elsie. O, yes! I see it now!

Prince Henry The grim musician
Leads all men through the mazes of that dance,
To different sounds in different measures moving;
Sometimes he plays a lute, sometimes a drum,
To tempt or terrify.

Elsie What is this picture?

Prince Henry It is a young man singing to a nun,
Who kneels at her devotions, but in kneeling
Turns round to look at him, and Death, meanwhile,
Is putting out the candles on the altar!

Elsie Ah, what a pity 't is that she should listen
to such songs, when in her orisons
She might have heard in heaven the angels singing!

Prince Henry Here he has stolen a jester's cap and bells,
And dances with the Queen.

Elsie A foolish jest!

Prince Henry And here the heart of the new-wedded wife,
Coming from church with her beloved lord,
He startles with the rattle of his drum.

Elsie Ah, that is sad! And yet perhaps 't is best
That she should die, with all the sunshine on her,

And all the benedictions of the morning,
Before this affluence of golden light
Shall fade into a cold and clouded gray,
Then into darkness!

Prince Henry Under it is written,
"Nothing but death shall separate thee and me!"

Elsie. And what is this, that follows close upon it?

Prince Henry Death, playing on a ducimer. Behind him,
A poor old woman, with a rosary,
Follows the sound, and seems to wish her feet
Were swifter to o'ertake him. Underneath,
The inscription reads, "Better is Death than Life."

Elsie. Better is Death than Life! Ah yes! to thousands
Death plays upon a dulcimer, and sings
That song of consolation, till the air
Rings with it, and they cannot choose but follow
Whither he leads. And not the old alone,
But the young also hear it, and are still.

Prince Henry Yes, in their sadder moments. 'T is the sound
Of their own hearts they hear, half full of tears,
Which are like crystal cups, half filled with water.
Responding to the pressure of a finger
With music sweet and low and melancholy.
Let us go forward, and no longer stay
In this great picture-gallery of Death!
I hate it! ay, the very thought of it!

Elsie. Why is it hateful to you?

Prince Henry. For the reason
That life, and all that speaks of life, is lovely,
And death, and all that speaks of death, is hateful.

Elsie. The grave is but a covered bridge,
leading from light to light, through a brief darkness!

Prince Henry (emerging from the bridge). I breathe again more
    freely! Ah, how pleasant
To come once more into the light of day,
Out of that shadow of death! To hear again
The hoof-beats of our horses on firm ground,
And not upon those hollow planks, resounding
With a sepulchral echo, like the clods
On coffins in a churchyard! Yonder lies
The Lake of the Four Forest-Towns, apparelled
In light, and lingering, like a village maiden,
Hid in the bosom of her native mountains,
Then pouring all her life into another's,
Changing her name and being! Overhead,
Shaking his cloudy tresses loose in air,
Rises Pilatus, with his windy pines.

    (They pass on.)

THE DEVIL'S BRIDGE.

PRINCE HENRY *and* ELSIE *crossing, with attendants.*

Guide. This bridge is called the Devil's Bridge.
With a single arch, from ridge to ridge,
It leaps across the terrible chasm
Yawning beneath us, black and deep,

As if, in some convulsive spasm,
the summits of the hills had cracked,
and made a road for the cataract,
That raves and rages down the steep!

  Lucifer (under the bridge). Ha! ha!

  Guide. Never any bridge but this
Could stand across the wild abyss;
All the rest, of wood or stone,
By the Devil's hand were overthrown.
He toppled crags from the precipice,
And whatsoe'er was built by day
In the night was swept away;
None could stand but this alone.

  Lucifer (under the bridge). Ha! ha!

  Guide. I showed you in the valley a boulder
Marked with the imprint of his shoulder;
As he was bearing it up this way,
A peasant, passing, cried, "Herr Je!"
And the Devil dropped it in his fright,
And vanished suddenly out of sight!

  Lucifer (under the bridge). Ha! ha!

  Guide. Abbot Giraldus of Einsiedel,
For pilgrims on their way to Rome,
Built this at last, with a single arch,
Under which, on its endless march,
Runs the river, white with foam,
Like a thread through the eye of a needle.

And the Devil promised to let it stand,
Under compact and condition
That the first living thing which crossed
Should be surrendered into his hand,
And be beyond redemption lost.
  Lucifer (under the bridge). Ha! ha! perdition!

Guide. At length, the bridge being all completed,
The Abbot, standing at its head,
Threw across it a loaf of bread,
Which a hungry dog sprang after,
And the rocks reechoed with peals of laughter
To see the Devil thus defeated!

    (They pass on)

  Lucifer (under the bridge) Ha! ha! defeated!
For journeys and for crimes like this
To let the bridge stand o'er the abyss!

THE ST. GOTHARD PASS.

  Prince Henry. This is the highest point. Two ways the rivers
Leap down to different seas, and as they roll
Grow deep and still, and their majestic presence
Becomes a benefaction to the towns
They visit, wandering silently among them,
Like patriarchs old among their shining tents.

  Elsie. How bleak and bare it is! Nothing but mosses
Grow on these rocks.

  Prince Henry. Yet are they not forgotten;

Beneficent Nature sends the mists to feed them.

Elsie. See yonder little cloud, that, borne aloft
So tenderly by the wind, floats fast away
Over the snowy peaks! It seems to me
The body of St. Catherine, borne by angels!

Prince Henry. Thou art St. Catherine, and invisible angels
Bear thee across these chasms and precipices,
Lest thou shouldst dash thy feet against a stone!

Elsie. Would I were borne unto my grave, as she was,
Upon angelic shoulders! Even now
I Seem uplifted by them, light as air!
What sound is that?

Prince Henry. The tumbling avalanches!

Elsie How awful, yet how beautiful!

Prince Henry. These are
The voices of the mountains! Thus they ope
Their snowy lips, and speak unto each other,
In the primeval language, lost to man.

Elsie. What land is this that spreads itself beneath us?

Prince Henry Italy! Italy!

Elsie Land of the Madonna!
How beautiful it is! It seems a garden
Of Paradise!

Prince Henry. Nay, of Gethsemane
To thee and me, of passion and of prayer!
Yet once of Paradise. Long years ago
I wandered as a youth among its bowers,
And never from my heart has faded quite
Its memory, that, like a summer sunset,
Encircles with a ring of purple light
All the horizon of my youth.

Guide. O friends!
The days are short, the way before us long;
We must not linger, if we think to reach
The inn at Belinzona before vespers!

(They pass on.)

AT THE FOOT OF THE ALPS.

A halt under the trees at noon.

Prince Henry Here let us pause a moment in the trembling
Shadow and sunshine of the roadside trees,
And, our tired horses in a group assembling,
Inhale long draughts of this delicious breeze
Our fleeter steeds have distanced our attendants;
They lag behind us with a slower pace;
We will await them under the green pendants
Of the great willows in this shady place.
Ho, Barbarossa! how thy mottled haunches
Sweat with this canter over hill and glade!
Stand still, and let these overhanging branches
Fan thy hot sides and comfort thee with shade!

Elsie. What a delightful landscape spreads before us,
Marked with a whitewashed cottage here and there!
And, in luxuriant garlands drooping o'er us,
Blossoms of grapevines scent the sunny air.

Prince Henry. Hark! what sweet sounds are those, whose accents holy
Fill the warm noon with music sad and sweet!

Elsie. It is a band of pilgrims, moving slowly
On their long journey, with uncovered feet.

Pilgrims (chaunting the Hymn of St. Hildebert)
    Me receptet Sion illa,
    Sion David, urbs tranquilla,
    Cujus faber auctor lucis,
    Cujus portae lignum crucis,
    Cujus claves lingua Petri,
    Cujus cives semper laeti,
    Cujus muri lapis vivus,
    Cujus custos Rex festivus!

Lucifer (as a Friar in the procession). Here am I, too, in the
    pious band,
In the garb of a barefooted Carmelite dressed!
The soles of my feet are as hard and tanned
As the conscience of old Pope Hildebrand,
The Holy Satan, who made the wives
Of the bishops lead such shameful lives.
All day long I beat my breast,
And chaunt with a most particular zest
The Latin hymns, which I understand
Quite as well, I think, as the rest.
And at night such lodging in barns and sheds,

Such a hurly-burly in country inns,
Such a clatter of tongues in empty heads,
Such a helter-skelter of prayers and sins!
Of all the contrivances of the time
For sowing broadcast the seeds of crime,
There is none so pleasing to me and mine
As a pilgrimage to some far-off shrine!

Prince Henry. If from the outward man we judge the inner,
And cleanliness is godliness, I fear
A hopeless reprobate, a hardened sinner,
Must be that Carmelite now passing near.

Lucifer. There is my German Prince again,
Thus far on his journey to Salern,
And the lovesick girl, whose heated brain
Is sowing the cloud to reap the rain;
But it's a long road that has no turn!
Let them quietly hold their way,
I have also a part in the play.
But first I must act to my heart's content
This mummery and this merriment,
And drive this motley flock of sheep
Into the fold, where drink and sleep
The jolly old friars of Benevent.
Of a truth, it often provokes me to laugh
To see these beggars hobble along,
Lamed and maimed, and fed upon chaff,
Chanting their wonderful piff and paff,
And, to make up for not understanding the song,
Singing it fiercely, and wild, and strong!
Were it not for my magic garters and staff,
And the goblets of goodly wine I quaff,

And the mischief I make in the idle throng,
I should not continue the business long.

    Pilgrims (chaunting). In hac uibe, lux solennis,
        Ver aeternum, pax perennis,
        In hac odor implens caelos,
        In hac semper festum melos!

Prince Henry. Do you observe that monk among the train,
Who pours from his great throat the roaring bass,
As a cathedral spout pours out the rain,
And this way turns his rubicund, round face?

Elsie. It is the same who, on the Strasburg square,
Preached to the people in the open air.

Prince Henry. And he has crossed o'er mountain, field, and fell,
On that good steed, that seems to bear him well,
The hackney of the Friars of Orders Gray,
His own stout legs! He, too, was in the play,
Both as King Herod and Ben Israel.
Good morrow, Friar!

Friar Cuthbert.   Good morrow, noble Sir!

Prince Henry. I speak in German, for, unless I err,
You are a German.

Friar Cuthbert. I cannot gainsay you.
But by what instinct, or what secret sign,
Meeting me here, do you straightway divine
That northward of the Alps my country lies?

The Golden Legend

Prince Henry. Your accent, like St, Peter's, would betray you,
Did not your yellow beard and your blue eyes,
Moreover, we have seen your face before,
And heard you preach at the Cathedral door
On Easter Sunday, in the Strasburg square
We were among the crowd that gathered there,
And saw you play the Rabbi with great skill,
As if, by leaning o'er so many years
To walk with little children, your own will
Had caught a childish attitude from theirs,
A kind of stooping in its form and gait,
And could no longer stand erect and straight.
Whence come you now?

Friar Cuthbert. From the old monastery
Of Hirschau, in the forest; being sent
Upon a pilgrimage to Benevent,
To see the image of the Virgin Mary,
That moves its holy eyes, and sometimes speaks,
And lets the piteous tears run down its cheeks,
To touch the hearts of the impenitent.

Prince Henry. O, had I faith, as in the days gone by,
That knew no doubt, and feared no mystery!

Lucifer (at a distance). Ho, Cuthbert! Friar Cuthbert!

Friar Cuthbert. Farewell, Prince!
I cannot stay to argue and convince.

Prince Henry. This is indeed the blessed Mary's land,
Virgin and Mother of our dear Redeemer!
All hearts are touched and softened at her name;

Alike the bandit, with the bloody hand,
The priest, the prince, the scholar, and the peasant,
The man of deeds, the visionary dreamer,
Pay homage to her as one ever present!
And even as children, who have much offended
A too indulgent father, in great shame,
Penitent, and yet not daring unattended
To go into his presence, at the gate
Speak with their sister, and confiding wait
Till she goes in before and intercedes;
So men, repenting of their evil deeds,
And yet not venturing rashly to draw near
With their requests an angry father's ear,
Offer to her their prayers and their confession,
And she for them in heaven makes intercession.
And if our Faith had given us nothing more
Than this example of all womanhood,
So mild, so merciful, so strong, so good,
So patient, peaceful, loyal, loving, pure,
This were enough to prove it higher and truer
Than all the creeds the world had known before.

Pilgrims (chaunting afar off). Urbs ccelestis, urbs beata,
    Supra petram collocata,
    Urbs in portu satis tuto
    De longinquo te saluto,
    Te saluto, te suspiro,
    Te affecto, te requiro!

THE INN AT GENOA.

A terrace overlooking the sea. Night.

Prince Henry. It is the sea, it is the sea,
In all its vague immensity,
Fading and darkening in the distance!
Silent, majestic, and slow,
The white ships haunt it to and fro,
With all their ghostly sails unfurled,
As phantoms from another world
Haunt the dim confines of existence!
But ah! how few can comprehend
Their signals, or to what good end
From land to land they come and go!
Upon a sea more vast and dark
The spirits of the dead embark,
All voyaging to unknown coasts.
We wave our farewells from the shore,
And they depart, and come no more,
Or come as phantoms and as ghosts.

Above the darksome sea of death
Looms the great life that is to be,
A land of cloud and mystery,
A dim mirage, with shapes of men
Long dead, and passed beyond our ken.
Awe-struck we gaze, and hold our breath
Till the fair pageant vanisheth,
Leaving us in perplexity,
And doubtful whether it has been
A vision of the world unseen,
Or a bright image of our own
Against the sky in vapors thrown.

   Lucifer (singing from the sea). Thou didst not make it, thou
      canst not mend it,

But thou hast the power to end it!
The sea is silent, the sea is discreet,
Deep it lies at thy very feet;
There is no confessor like unto Death!
Thou canst not see him, but he is near;
Thou needest not whisper above thy breath,
And he will hear;
He will answer the questions,
The vague surmises and suggestions,
That fill thy soul with doubt and fear!

Prince Henry. The fisherman, who lies afloat,
With shadowy sail, in yonder boat,
Is singing softly to the Night!
But do I comprehend aright
The meaning of the words he sung
So sweetly in his native tongue?
Ah, yes! the sea is still and deep.
All things within its bosom sleep!
A single step, and all is o'er;
A plunge, a bubble, and no more;
And thou, dear Elsie, wilt be free
From martyrdom and agony.

Elsie (coming from her chamber upon the terrace).
The night is calm and cloudless,
And still as still can be,
And the stars come forth to listen
To the music of the sea.
They gather, and gather, and gather,
Until they crowd the sky,
And listen, in breathless silence,
To the solemn litany.

It begins in rocky caverns,
As a voice that chaunts alone
To the pedals of the organ
In monotonous undertone;
And anon from shelving beaches,
And shallow sands beyond,
In snow-white robes uprising
The ghostly choirs respond.
And sadly and unceasing
The mournful voice sings on,
And the snow-white choirs still answer
Christe eleison!

Prince Henry. Angel of God! thy finer sense perceives
Celestial and perpetual harmonies!
Thy purer soul, that trembles and believes,
Hears the archangel's trumpet in the breeze,
And where the forest rolls, or ocean heaves,
Cecilia's organ sounding in the seas,
And tongues of prophets speaking in the leaves.
But I hear discord only and despair,
And whispers as of demons in the air!

AT SEA.

Il Padrone. The wind upon our quarter lies,
And on before the freshening gale,
That fills the snow-white lateen sail,
Swiftly our light felucca flies.
Around, the billows burst and foam;
They lift her o'er the sunken rock,
They beat her sides with many a shock,
And then upon their flowing dome

They poise her, like a weathercock!
Between us and the western skies
The hills of Corsica arise;
Eastward, in yonder long, blue line,
The summits of the Apennine,
And southward, and still far away,
Salerno, on its sunny bay.
You cannot see it, where it lies.

Prince Henry. Ah, would that never more mine eyes
Might see its towers by night or day!

Elsie. Behind us, dark and awfully,
There comes a cloud out of the sea,
That bears the form of a hunted deer,
With hide of brown, and hoofs of black,
And antlers laid upon its back,
And fleeing fast and wild with fear,
As if the hounds were on its track!

Prince Henry. Lo! while we gaze, it breaks and falls
In shapeless masses, like the walls
Of a burnt city. Broad and red
The fires of the descending sun
Glare through the windows, and o'erhead,
Athwart the vapors, dense and dun,
Long shafts of silvery light arise,
Like rafters that support the skies!

Elsie. See! from its summit the lurid levin
Flashes downward without warning,
As Lucifer, son of the morning,
Fell from the battlements of heaven!

Il Padrone. I must entreat you, friends, below!
The angry storm begins to blow,
For the weather changes with the moon.
All this morning, until noon,
We had baffling winds, and sudden flaws
Struck the sea with their cat's-paws.
Only a little hour ago
I was whistling to Saint Antonio
For a capful of wind to fill our sail,
And instead of a breeze he has sent a gale.
Last night I saw St. Elmo's stars,
With their glimmering lanterns, all at play
On the tops of the masts and the tips of the spars,
And I knew we should have foul weather to-day.
Cheerily, my hearties! yo heave ho!
Brail up the mainsail, and let her go
As the winds will and Saint Antonio!

Do you see that Livornese felucca,
That vessel to the windward yonder,
Running with her gunwale under?
I was looking when the wind o'ertook her,
She had all sail set, and the only wonder
Is that at once the strength of the blast
Did not carry away her mast.
She is a galley of the Gran Duca,
That, through the fear of the Algerines,
Convoys those lazy brigantines,
Laden with wine and oil from Lucca.
Now all is ready, high and low;
Blow, blow, good Saint Antonio!

Ha! that is the first dash of the rain,

With a sprinkle of spray above the rails,
Just enough to moisten our sails,
And make them ready for the strain.
See how she leaps, as the blasts o'ertake her,
And speeds away with a bone in her mouth!
Now keep her head toward the south,
And there is no danger of bank or breaker.
With the breeze behind us, on we go;
Not too much, good Saint Antonio!

VI. THE SCHOOL OF SALERNO.

A traveling Scholastic affixing his Theses to the gate of the College.

  Scholastic. There, that is my gauntlet, my banner, my shield,
Hung up as a challenge to all the field!
One hundred and twenty-five propositions,
Which I will maintain with the sword of the tongue
Against all disputants, old and young.
Let us see if doctors or dialecticians
Will dare to dispute my definitions,
Or attack any one of my learned theses.
Here stand I; the end shall be as God pleases.
I think I have proved, by profound research
The error of all those doctrines so vicious
Of the old Areopagite Dionysius,
That are making such terrible work in the churches,
By Michael the Stammerer sent from the East,
And done into Latin by that Scottish beast,
Erigena Johannes, who dares to maintain,
In the face of the truth, the error infernal,
That the universe is and must be eternal;
At first laying down, as a fact fundamental,
That nothing with God can be accidental;
Then asserting that God before the creation

Could not have existed, because it is plain
That, had he existed, he would have created;
Which is begging the question that should be debated,
And moveth me less to anger than laughter.
All nature, he holds, is a respiration
Of the Spirit of God, who, in breathing, hereafter
Will inhale it into his bosom again,
So that nothing but God alone will remain.
And therein he contradicteth himself;
For he opens the whole discussion by stating,
That God can only exist in creating.
That question I think I have laid on the shelf!

> (He goes out. Two Doctors come in disputing, and followed by pupils.)

Doctor Serafino. I, with the Doctor Seraphic, maintain,
That a word which is only conceived in the brain
Is a type of eternal Generation;
The spoken word is the Incarnation.

Doctor Cherubino. What do I care for the Doctor Seraphic,
With all his wordy chaffer and traffic?

Doctor Serafino. You make but a paltry show of resistance;
Universals have no real existence!

Doctor Cherubino. Your words are but idle and empty chatter;
Ideas are eternally joined to matter!

Doctor Serafino. May the Lord have mercy on your position,
You wretched, wrangling culler of herbs!

Doctor Cherubino. May he send your soul to eternal perdition,
For your Treatise on the Irregular Verbs!

(They rush out fighting. Two Scholars come in.)

First Scholar. Monte Cassino, then, is your College.
What think you of ours here at Salern?

Second Scholar. To tell the truth, I arrived so lately,
I hardly yet have had time to discern.
So much, at least, I am bound to acknowledge:
The air seems healthy, the buildings stately,
And on the whole I like it greatly.

First Scholar. Yes, the air is sweet; the Calabrian hills
Send us down puffs of mountain air;
And in summer time the sea-breeze fills
With its coolness cloister, and court, and square.
Then at every season of the year
There are crowds of guests and travellers here;
Pilgrims, and mendicant friars, and traders
From the Levant, with figs and wine,
And bands of wounded and sick Crusaders,
Coming back from Palestine.

Second Scholar. And what are the studies you pursue?
What is the course you here go through?

First Scholar. The first three years of the college course
Are given to Logic alone, as the source
Of all that is noble, and wise, and true.

Second Scholar. That seems rather strange, I must confess.

In a Medical School; yet, nevertheless,
You doubtless have reasons for that.

First Scholar. Oh yes!
For none but a clever dialectician
Can hope to become a great physician;
That has been settled long ago.
Logic makes an important part
Of the mystery of the healing art;
For without it how could you hope to show
That nobody knows so much as you know?
After this there are five years more
Devoted wholly to medicine,
With lectures on chirurgical lore,
And dissections of the bodies of swine,
As likest the human form divine.

Second Scholar. What are the books now most in vogue?

First Scholar. Quite an extensive catalogue;
Mostly, however, books of our own;
As Gariopontus' Passionarius,
And the writings of Matthew Platearius;
And a volume universally known
As the Regimen of the School of Salern,
For Robert of Normandy written in terse
And very elegant Latin verse.
Each of these writings has its turn.
And when at length we have finished these,
Then comes the struggle for degrees,
With all the oldest and ablest critics;
The public thesis and disputation,
Question, and answer, and explanation

Of a passage out of Hippocrates,
Or Aristotle's Analytics.
There the triumphant Magister stands!
A book is solemnly placed in his hands,
On which he swears to follow the rule
And ancient forms of the good old School;
To report if any confectionarius
Mingles his drugs with matters various,
And to visit his patients twice a day,
And once in the night, if they live in town,
And if they are poor, to take no pay.
Having faithfully promised these,
His head is crowned with a laurel crown;
A kiss on his cheek, a ring on his hand,
The Magister Artium et Physices
Goes forth from the school like a lord of the land.
And now, as we have the whole morning before us
Let us go in, if you make no objection,
And listen awhile to a learned prelection
On Marcus Aurelius Cassiodorus.

(They go in. Enter LUCIFER *as a Doctor.*)

Lucifer. This is the great School of Salern!
A land of wrangling and of quarrels,
Of brains that seethe, and hearts that burn,
Where every emulous scholar hears,
In every breath that comes to his ears,
The rustling of another's laurels!
The air of the place is called salubrious;
The neighborhood of Vesuvius lends it
An odor volcanic, that rather mends it,
And the buildings have an aspect lugubrious,

That inspires a feeling of awe and terror
Into the heart of the beholder,
And befits such an ancient homestead of error,
Where the old falsehoods moulder and smoulder,
And yearly by many hundred hands
Are carried away, in the zeal of youth,
And sown like tares in the field of truth,
To blossom and ripen in other lands.
What have we here, affixed to the gate?
The challenge of some scholastic wight,
Who wishes to hold a public debate
On sundry questions wrong or right!
Ah, now this is my great delight!
For I have often observed of late
That such discussions end in a fight.
Let us see what the learned wag maintains
With such a prodigal waste of brains.

(Reads.)

"Whether angels in moving from place to place
Pass through the intermediate space.
Whether God himself is the author of evil,
Or whether that is the work of the Devil.
When, where, and wherefore Lucifer fell,
And whether he now is chained in hell."

I think I can answer that question well!
So long as the boastful human mind
Consents in such mills as this to grind,
I sit very firmly upon my throne!
Of a truth it almost makes me laugh,
To see men leaving the golden grain

To gather in piles the pitiful chaff
That old Peter Lombard thrashed with his brain,
To have it caught up and tossed again
On the horns of the Dumb Ox of Cologne!

But my guests approach! there is in the air
A fragrance, like that of the Beautiful Garden
Of Paradise, in the days that were!
An odor of innocence, and of prayer,
And of love, and faith that never fails,
Which as the fresh-young heart exhales
Before it begins to wither and harden!
I cannot breathe such an atmosphere!
My soul is filled with a nameless fear,
That, after all my trouble and pain,
After all my restless endeavor,
The youngest, fairest soul of the twain,
The most ethereal, most divine,
Will escape from my hands forever and ever.
But the other is already mine!
Let him live to corrupt his race,
Breathing among them, with every breath,
Weakness, selfishness, and the base
And pusillanimous fear of death.
I know his nature, and I know
That of all who in my ministry
Wander the great earth to and fro,
And on my errands come and go,
The safest and subtlest are such as he.

 (Enter PRINCE HENRY *and* ELSIE *with
  attendants*.)

Prince Henry. Can you direct us to Friar Angelo?

Lucifer. He stands before you.

Prince Henry. Then you know our purpose.
I am Prince Henry of Hoheneck, and this
The maiden that I spake of in my letters.

Lucifer. It is a very grave and solemn business!
We must not be precipitate. Does she
Without compulsion, of her own free will,
Consent to this?

Prince Henry. Against all opposition,
Against all prayers, entreaties, protestations.
She will not be persuaded.

Lucifer. That is strange!
Have you thought well of it?

Elsie. I come not here
To argue, but to die. Your business is not
to question, but to kill me. I am ready.
I am impatient to be gone from here
Ere any thoughts of earth disturb again
The spirit of tranquillity within me.

Prince Henry. Would I had not come here
 Would I were dead,
And thou wert in thy cottage in the forest,
And hadst not known me! Why have I done this?
Let me go back and die.

The Golden Legend

Elsie. It cannot be;
Not if these cold, flat stones on which we tread
Were coulters heated white, and yonder gateway
Flamed like a furnace with a sevenfold heat.
I must fulfil my purpose.

Prince Henry. I forbid it!
Not one step farther. For I only meant
To put thus far thy courage to the proof.
It is enough. I, too, have courage to die,
For thou hast taught me!

Elsie. O my Prince! remember
Your promises. Let me fulfill my errand.
You do not look on life and death as I do.
There are two angels, that attend unseen
Each one of us, and in great books record
Our good and evil deeds. He who writes down
The good ones, after every action closes
His volume, and ascends with it to God.
The other keeps his dreadful day-book open
Till sunset, that we may repent; which doing,
The record of the action fades away,
And leaves a line of white across the page.
Now if my act be good, as I believe it,
It cannot be recalled. It is already
Sealed up in heaven, as a good deed accomplished.
The rest is yours. Why wait you? I am ready.

(To her attendants.)

Weep not, my friends! rather rejoice with me.
I shall not feel the pain, but shall be gone,

And you will have another friend in heaven.
Then start not at the creaking of the door
Through which I pass. I see what lies beyond it.

(To PRINCE HENRY.)

And you, O Prince! bear back my benison
Unto my father's house, and all within it.
This morning in the church I prayed for them,
After confession, after absolution,
When my whole soul was white, I prayed for them.
God will take care of them, they need me not.
And in your life let my remembrance linger,
As something not to trouble and disturb it,
But to complete it, adding life to life.
And if at times beside the evening fire
You see my face among the other faces,
Let it not be regarded as a ghost
That haunts your house, but as a guest that loves you.
Nay, even as one of your own family,
Without whose presence there were something wanting.
I have no more to say. Let us go in.

Prince Henry. Friar Angelo! I charge you on your life,
Believe not what she says, for she is mad,
And comes here not to die, but to be healed.

Elsie. Alas! Prince Henry!

Lucifer. Come with me; this way.

(ELSIE *goes in with* LUCIFER, *who thrusts* PRINCE HENRY *back and closes the door.*)

Prince Henry. Gone! and the light of all my life gone with her!
A sudden darkness falls upon the world!

Forester. News from the Prince!

Ursula. Of death or life?

Forester. You put your questions eagerly!

Ursula. Answer me, then! How is the Prince?

Forester. I left him only two hours since
Homeward returning down the river,
As strong and well as if God, the Giver,
Had given him back in his youth again.

Ursula (despairing). Then Elsie, my poor child, is dead!

Forester. That, my good woman, I have not said.
Don't cross the bridge till you come to it,
Is a proverb old, and of excellent wit.

Ursula. Keep me no longer in this pain!

Forester. It is true your daughter is no more;--
That is, the peasant she was before.

Ursula. Alas! I am simple and lowly bred
I am poor, distracted, and forlorn.
And it is not well that you of the court
Should mock me thus, and make a sport
Of a joyless mother whose child is dead,

For you, too, were of mother, born!

Forester. Your daughter lives, and the Prince is well!
You will learn ere long how it all befell.
Her heart for a moment never failed;
But when they reached Salerno's gate,
The Prince's nobler self prevailed,
And saved her for a nobler fate,
And he was healed, in his despair,
By the touch of St. Matthew's sacred bones;
Though I think the long ride in the open air,
That pilgrimage over stocks and stones,
In the miracle must come in for a share!

Ursula. Virgin! who lovest the poor and lonely,
If the loud cry of a mother's heart
Can ever ascend to where thou art,
Into thy blessed hands and holy
Receive my prayer of praise and thanksgiving!
Let the hands that bore our Saviour bear it
Into the awful presence of God;
For thy feet with holiness are shod,
And if thou bearest it he will hear it.
Our child who was dead again is living!

Forester. I did not tell you she was dead;
If you thought so 'twas no fault of mine;
At this very moment, while I speak,
They are sailing homeward down the Rhine,
In a splendid barge, with golden prow,
And decked with banners white and red
As the colors on your daughter's cheek.
They call her the Lady Alicia now;

For the Prince in Salerno made a vow
That Elsie only would he wed.

Ursula. Jesu Maria! what a change!
All seems to me so weird and strange!

Forester. I saw her standing on the deck,
Beneath an awning cool and shady;
Her cap of velvet could not hold
The tresses of her hair of gold,
That flowed and floated like the stream,
And fell in masses down her neck.
As fair and lovely did she seem
As in a story or a dream
Some beautiful and foreign lady.
And the Prince looked so grand and proud,
And waved his hand thus to the crowd
That gazed and shouted from the shore,
All down the river, long and loud.

Ursula. We shall behold our child once more;
She is not dead! She is not dead!
God, listening, must have overheard
The prayers, that, without sound or word,
Our hearts in secrecy have said!
O, bring me to her; for mine eyes
Are hungry to behold her face;
My very soul within me cries;
My very hands seem to caress her,
To see her, gaze at her, and bless her;
Dear Elsie, child of God and grace!

(Goes out toward the garden.)

Forester. There goes the good woman out of her head;
And Gottlieb's supper is waiting here;
A very capacious flagon of beer,
And a very portentous loaf of bread.
One would say his grief did not much oppress him.
Here's to the health of the Prince, God bless him!

(He drinks.)

Ha! it buzzes and stings like a hornet!
And what a scene there, through the door!
The forest behind and the garden before,
And midway an old man of threescore,
With a wife and children that caress him.
Let me try still further to cheer and adorn it
With a merry, echoing blast of my cornet!

(Goes out blowing his horn.)

THE CASTLE OF VAUTSBERG ON THE RHINE.

PRINCE HENRY *and* ELSIE *standing on the terrace at evening. The sound of bells heard from a distance.*

Prince Henry. We are alone. The wedding guests
Ride down the hill, with plumes and cloaks,
And the descending dark invests
The Niederwald, and all the nests
Among its hoar and haunted oaks.

Elsie. What bells are those, that ring so slow,
So mellow, musical, and low?

Prince Henry. They are the bells of Geisenheim,
That with their melancholy chime
Ring out the curfew of the sun.

Elsie. Listen, beloved.

Prince Henry. They are done!
Dear Elsie! many years ago
Those same soft bells at eventide
Rang in the ears of Charlemagne,
As, seated by Fastrada's side
At Ingelheim, in all his pride
He heard their sound with secret pain.

Elsie. Their voices only speak to me
Of peace and deep tranquillity,
And endless confidence in thee!

Prince Henry. Thou knowest the story of her ring,
How, when the court went back to Aix,
Fastrada died; and how the king
Sat watching by her night and day,
Till into one of the blue lakes,
That water that delicious land,
They cast the ring, drawn from her hand;
And the great monarch sat serene
And sad beside the fated shore,
Nor left the land forever more.

Elsie. That was true love.

Prince Henry. For him the queen
Ne'er did what thou hast done for me.

Elsie. Wilt thou as fond and faithful be?
Wilt thou so love me after death?

Prince Henry. In life's delight, in death's dismay,
In storm and sunshine, night and day,
In health, in sickness, in decay,
Here and hereafter, I am thine!
Thou hast Fastrada's ring. Beneath
The calm, blue waters of thine eyes
Deep in thy steadfast soul it lies,
And, undisturbed by this world's breath,
With magic light its jewels shine!
This golden ring, which thou hast worn
Upon thy finger since the morn,
Is but a symbol and a semblance,
An outward fashion, a remembrance,
Of what thou wearest within unseen,
O my Fastrada, O my queen!
Behold! the hilltops all aglow
With purple and with amethyst;
While the whole valley deep below
Is filled, and seems to overflow,
With a fast-rising tide of mist.
The evening air grows damp and chill;
Let us go in.

Elsie. Ah, not so soon.
See yonder fire! It is the moon
Slow rising o'er the eastern hill.
It glimmers on the forest tips,
And through the dewy foliage drips
In little rivulets of light,
And makes the heart in love with night.

Prince Henry. Oft on this terrace, when the day
Was closing, have I stood and gazed,
And seen the landscape fade away,
And the white vapors rise and drown
Hamlet and vineyard, tower and town
While far above the hilltops blazed.
But men another hand than thine
Was gently held and clasped in mine;
Another head upon my breast
Was laid, as thine is now, at rest.
Why dost thou lift those tender eyes
With so much sorrow and surprise?
A minstrel's, not a maiden's hand,
Was that which in my own was pressed.
A manly form usurped thy place,
A beautiful, but bearded face,
That now is in the Holy Land,
Yet in my memory from afar
Is shining on us like a star.
But linger not. For while I speak,
A sheeted spectre white and tall,
The cold mist climbs the castle wall,
And lays his hand upon thy cheek!

   (They go in.)

EPILOGUE.

THE TWO RECORDING ANGELS ASCENDING.

 The Angel of Good Deeds (with closed book). God sent his
  messenger the rain,
And said unto the mountain brook,
"Rise up, and from thy caverns look
And leap, with naked, snow-white feet.
From the cool hills into the heat
Of the broad, arid plain."

God sent his messenger of faith,
And whispered in the maiden's heart,
"Rise up, and look from where thou art,
And scatter with unselfish hands
Thy freshness on the barren sands
And solitudes of Death."
O beauty of holiness,
Of self-forgetfulness, of lowliness!
O power of meekness,
Whose very gentleness and weakness
Are like the yielding, but irresistible air!
Upon the pages
Of the sealed volume that I bear,

The deed divine
Is written in characters of gold,
That never shall grow old,
But all through ages
Burn and shine,
With soft effulgence!
O God! it is thy indulgence
That fills the world with the bliss
Of a good deed like this!

   The Angel of Evil Deeds (with open book). Not yet, not yet
Is the red sun wholly set,
But evermore recedes,
While open still I bear
The Book of Evil Deeds,
To let the breathings of the upper air
Visit its pages and erase
The records from its face!
Fainter and fainter as I gaze
On the broad blaze
The glimmering landscape shines,
And below me the black river
Is hidden by wreaths of vapor!
Fainter and fainter the black lines
Begin to quiver
Along the whitening surface of the paper;
Shade after shade
The terrible words grow faint and fade,
And in their place
Runs a white space!

Down goes the sun!
But the soul of one,

Who by repentance
Has escaped the dreadful sentence,
Shines bright below me as I look.
It is the end!
With closed Book
To God do I ascend.

Lo! over the mountain steeps
A dark, gigantic shadow sweeps
Beneath my feet;
A blackness inwardly brightening
With sullen heat,
As a storm-cloud lurid with lightning.
And a cry of lamentation,
Repeated and again repeated,
Deep and loud
As the reverberation
Of cloud answering unto cloud,
Swells and rolls away in the distance,
As if the sheeted
Lightning retreated,
Baffled and thwarted by the wind's resistance.

It is Lucifer,
The son of mystery;
And since God suffers him to be,
He, too, is God's minister,
And labors for some good
By us not understood!

www.bookjungle.com email: sales@bookjungle.com fax: 630-214-0564 mail: Book Jungle PO Box 2226 Champaign, IL 61825

The Codes Of Hammurabi And Moses
W. W. Davies

QTY

The discovery of the Hammurabi Code is one of the greatest achievements of archaeology, and is of paramount interest, not only to the student of the Bible, but also to all those interested in ancient history...

Religion   ISBN: *1-59462-338-4*   Pages:132
                                            MSRP *$12.95*

The Theory of Moral Sentiments
Adam Smith

QTY

This work from 1749. contains original theories of conscience amd moral judgment and it is the foundation for systemof morals.

Philosophy   ISBN: *1-59462-777-0*   Pages:536
                                            MSRP *$19.95*

Jessica's First Prayer
Hesba Stretton

QTY

In a screened and secluded corner of one of the many railway-bridges which span the streets of London there could be seen a few years ago, from five o'clock every morning until half past eight, a tidily set-out coffee-stall, consisting of a trestle and board, upon which stood two large tin cans, with a small fire of charcoal burning under each so as to keep the coffee boiling during the early hours of the morning when the work-people were thronging into the city on their way to their daily toil...

Childrens   ISBN: *1-59462-373-2*   Pages:84
                                            MSRP *$9.95*

My Life and Work
Henry Ford

QTY

Henry Ford revolutionized the world with his implementation of mass production for the Model T automobile. Gain valuable business insight into his life and work with his own auto-biography... "We have only started on our development of our country we have not as yet, with all our talk of wonderful progress, done more than scratch the surface. The progress has been wonderful enough but..."

Biographies/ ISBN: *1-59462-198-5*   Pages:300
                                            MSRP *$21.95*

www.bookjungle.com email: sales@bookjungle.com fax: 630-214-0564 mail: Book Jungle PO Box 2226 Champaign, IL 61825

The Art of Cross-Examination
Francis Wellman

QTY

I presume it is the experience of every author, after his first book is published upon an important subject, to be almost overwhelmed with a wealth of ideas and illustrations which could readily have been included in his book, and which to his own mind, at least, seem to make a second edition inevitable. Such certainly was the case with me; and when the first edition had reached its sixth impression in five months, I rejoiced to learn that it seemed to my publishers that the book had met with a sufficiently favorable reception to justify a second and considerably enlarged edition. ..

Reference   ISBN: *1-59462-647-2*   Pages:412 MSRP *$19.95*

On the Duty of Civil Disobedience
Henry David Thoreau

QTY

Thoreau wrote his famous essay, On the Duty of Civil Disobedience, as a protest against an unjust but popular war and the immoral but popular institution of slave-owning. He did more than write—he declined to pay his taxes, and was hauled off to gaol in consequence. Who can say how much this refusal of his hastened the end of the war and of slavery ?

Law   ISBN: *1-59462-747-9*   Pages:48 MSRP *$7.45*

Dream Psychology Psychoanalysis for Beginners
Sigmund Freud

QTY

Sigmund Freud, born Sigismund Schlomo Freud (May 6, 1856 - September 23, 1939), was a Jewish-Austrian neurologist and psychiatrist who co-founded the psychoanalytic school of psychology. Freud is best known for his theories of the unconscious mind, especially involving the mechanism of repression; his redefinition of sexual desire as mobile and directed towards a wide variety of objects; and his therapeutic techniques, especially his understanding of transference in the therapeutic relationship and the presumed value of dreams as sources of insight into unconscious desires.

Psychology   ISBN: *1-59462-905-6*   Pages:196 MSRP *$15.45*

The Miracle of Right Thought
Orison Swett Marden

QTY

Believe with all of your heart that you will do what you were made to do. When the mind has once formed the habit of holding cheerful, happy, prosperous pictures, it will not be easy to form the opposite habit. It does not matter how improbable or how far away this realization may see, or how dark the prospects may be, if we visualize them as best we can, as vividly as possible, hold tenaciously to them and vigorously struggle to attain them, they will gradually become actualized, realized in the life. But a desire, a longing without endeavor, a yearning abandoned or held indifferently will vanish without realization.

Self Help   ISBN: *1-59462-644-8*   Pages:360 MSRP *$25.45*

www.bookjungle.com *email: sales@bookjungle.com fax: 630-214-0564 mail: Book Jungle PO Box 2226 Champaign, IL 61825*

QTY

☐ **The Rosicrucian Cosmo-Conception Mystic Christianity** *by Max Heindel* ISBN: *1-59462-188-8* **$38.95**
The Rosicrucian Cosmo-conception is not dogmatic, neither does it appeal to any other authority than the reason of the student. It is: not controversial, but is: sent forth in the, hope that it may help to clear... New Age/Religion Pages 646

☐ **Abandonment To Divine Providence** *by Jean-Pierre de Caussade* ISBN: *1-59462-228-0* **$25.95**
"The Rev. Jean Pierre de Caussade was one of the most remarkable spiritual writers of the Society of Jesus in France in the 18th Century. His death took place at Toulouse in 1751. His works have gone through many editions and have been republished... Inspirational/Religion Pages 400

☐ **Mental Chemistry** *by Charles Haanel* ISBN: *1-59462-192-6* **$23.95**
Mental Chemistry allows the change of material conditions by combining and appropriately utilizing the power of the mind. Much like applied chemistry creates something new and unique out of careful combinations of chemicals the mastery of mental chemistry... New Age Pages 354

☐ **The Letters of Robert Browning and Elizabeth Barret Barrett 1845-1846 vol II** ISBN: *1-59462-193-4* **$35.95**
by Robert Browning and Elizabeth Barrett Biographies Pages 596

☐ **Gleanings In Genesis (volume I)** *by Arthur W. Pink* ISBN: *1-59462-130-6* **$27.45**
Appropriately has Genesis been termed "the seed plot of the Bible" for in it we have, in germ form, almost all of the great doctrines which are afterwards fully developed in the books of Scripture which follow... Religion/Inspirational Pages 420

☐ **The Master Key** *by L. W. de Laurence* ISBN: *1-59462-001-6* **$30.95**
In no branch of human knowledge has there been a more lively increase of the spirit of research during the past few years than in the study of Psychology, Concentration and Mental Discipline. The requests for authentic lessons in Thought Control, Mental Discipline and... New Age/Business Pages 422

☐ **The Lesser Key Of Solomon Goetia** *by L. W. de Laurence* ISBN: *1-59462-092-X* **$9.95**
This translation of the first book of the "Lernegton" which is now for the first time made accessible to students of Talismanic Magic was done, after careful collation and edition, from numerous Ancient Manuscripts in Hebrew, Latin, and French... New Age/Occult Pages 92

☐ **Rubaiyat Of Omar Khayyam** *by Edward Fitzgerald* ISBN: *1-59462-332-5* **$13.95**
Edward Fitzgerald, whom the world has already learned, in spite of his own efforts to remain within the shadow of anonymity, to look upon as one of the rarest poets of the century, was born at Bredfield, in Suffolk, on the 31st of March, 1809. He was the third son of John Purcell... Music Pages 172

☐ **Ancient Law** *by Henry Maine* ISBN: *1-59462-128-4* **$29.95**
The chief object of the following pages is to indicate some of the earliest ideas of mankind, as they are reflected in Ancient Law, and to point out the relation of those ideas to modern thought. Religion/History Pages 452

☐ **Far-Away Stories** *by William J. Locke* ISBN: *1-59462-129-2* **$19.45**
"Good wine needs no bush, but a collection of mixed vintages does. And this book is just such a collection. Some of the stories I do not want to remain buried for ever in the museum files of dead magazine-numbers an author's not unpardonable vanity..." Fiction Pages 272

☐ **Life of David Crockett** *by David Crockett* ISBN: *1-59462-250-7* **$27.45**
"Colonel David Crockett was one of the most remarkable men of the times in which he lived. Born in humble life, but gifted with a strong will, an indomitable courage, and unremitting perseverance... Biographies/New Age Pages 424

☐ **Lip-Reading** *by Edward Nitchie* ISBN: *1-59462-206-X* **$25.95**
Edward B. Nitchie, founder of the New York School for the Hard of Hearing, now the Nitchie School of Lip-Reading, Inc, wrote "LIP-READING Principles and Practice". The development and perfecting of this meritorious work on lip-reading was an undertaking... How-to/Health Pages 400

☐ **A Handbook of Suggestive Therapeutics, Applied Hypnotism, Psychic Science** ISBN: *1-59462-214-0* **$24.95**
by Henry Munro Health/New Age/Health/Self-help Pages 376

☐ **A Doll's House: and Two Other Plays** *by Henrik Ibsen* ISBN: *1-59462-112-8* **$19.95**
Henrik Ibsen created this classic when in revolutionary 1848 Rome. Introducing some striking concepts in playwriting for the realist genre, this play has been studied the world over. Fiction/Classics/Plays 308

☐ **The Light of Asia** *by sir Edwin Arnold* ISBN: *1-59462-204-3* **$13.95**
In this poetic masterpiece, Edwin Arnold describes the life and teachings of Buddha. The man who was to become known as Buddha to the world was born as Prince Gautama of India but he rejected the worldly riches and abandoned the reigns of power when... Religion/History/Biographies Pages 170

☐ **The Complete Works of Guy de Maupassant** *by Guy de Maupassant* ISBN: *1-59462-157-8* **$16.95**
"For days and days, nights and nights, I had dreamed of that first kiss which was to consecrate our engagement, and I knew not on what spot I should put my lips..." Fiction/Classics Pages 240

☐ **The Art of Cross-Examination** *by Francis L. Wellman* ISBN: *1-59462-309-0* **$26.95**
Written by a renowned trial lawyer, Wellman imparts his experience and uses case studies to explain how to use psychology to extract desired information through questioning. How-to/Science/Reference Pages 408

☐ **Answered or Unanswered?** *by Louisa Vaughan* ISBN: *1-59462-248-5* **$10.95**
Miracles of Faith in China Religion Pages 112

☐ **The Edinburgh Lectures on Mental Science (1909)** *by Thomas* ISBN: *1-59462-008-3* **$11.95**
This book contains the substance of a course of lectures recently given by the writer in the Queen Street Hall, Edinburgh. Its purpose is to indicate the Natural Principles governing the relation between Mental Action and Material Conditions... New Age/Psychology Pages 148

☐ **Ayesha** *by H. Rider Haggard* ISBN: *1-59462-301-5* **$24.95**
Verily and indeed it is the unexpected that happens! Probably if there was one person upon the earth from whom the Editor of this, and of a certain previous history, did not expect to hear again... Classics Pages 380

☐ **Ayala's Angel** *by Anthony Trollope* ISBN: *1-59462-352-X* **$29.95**
The two girls were both pretty, but Lucy who was twenty-one who supposed to be simple and comparatively unattractive, whereas Ayala was credited, as her Bombwhat romantic name might show, with poetic charm and a taste for romance. Ayala when her father died was nineteen... Fiction Pages 484

☐ **The American Commonwealth** *by James Bryce* ISBN: *1-59462-286-8* **$34.45**
An interpretation of American democratic political theory. It examines political mechanics and society from the perspective of Scotsman James Bryce Politics Pages 572

☐ **Stories of the Pilgrims** *by Margaret P. Pumphrey* ISBN: *1-59462-116-0* **$17.95**
This book explores pilgrims religious oppression in England as well as their escape to Holland and eventual crossing to America on the Mayflower, and their early days in New England... History Pages 268

www.bookjungle.com *email: sales@bookjungle.com fax: 630-214-0564 mail: Book Jungle PO Box 2226 Champaign, IL 61825*

QTY

The Fasting Cure *by Sinclair Upton*   ISBN: *1-59462-222-1*   **$13.95**
In the Cosmopolitan Magazine for May, 1910, and in the Contemporary Review (London) for April, 1910, I published an article dealing with my experiences in fasting. I have written a great many magazine articles, but never one which attracted so much attention...   *New Age/Self Help/Health Pages 164*

Hebrew Astrology *by Sepharial*   ISBN: *1-59462-308-2*   **$13.45**
In these days of advanced thinking it is a matter of common observation that we have left many of the old landmarks behind and that we are now pressing forward to greater heights and to a wider horizon than that which represented the mind-content of our progenitors...   *Astrology Pages 144*

Thought Vibration or The Law of Attraction in the Thought World   ISBN: *1-59462-127-6*   **$12.95**
by William Walker Atkinson   *Psychology/Religion Pages 144*

Optimism *by Helen Keller*   ISBN: *1-59462-108-X*   **$15.95**
Helen Keller was blind, deaf, and mute since 19 months old, yet famously learned how to overcome these handicaps, communicate with the world, and spread her lectures promoting optimism. An inspiring read for everyone...   *Biographies/Inspirational Pages 84*

Sara Crewe *by Frances Burnett*   ISBN: *1-59462-360-0*   **$9.45**
In the first place, Miss Minchin lived in London. Her home was a large, dull, tall one, in a large, dull square, where all the houses were alike, and all the sparrows were alike, and where all the door-knockers made the same heavy sound...   *Childrens/Classic Pages 88*

The Autobiography of Benjamin Franklin *by Benjamin Franklin*   ISBN: *1-59462-135-7*   **$24.95**
The Autobiography of Benjamin Franklin has probably been more extensively read than any other American historical work, and no other book of its kind has had such ups and downs of fortune. Franklin lived for many years in England, where he was agent...   *Biographies/History Pages 332*

Name	
Email	
Telephone	
Address	
City, State ZIP	

☐ Credit Card   ☐ Check / Money Order

Credit Card Number	
Expiration Date	
Signature	

Please Mail to: Book Jungle
PO Box 2226
Champaign, IL 61825
or Fax to: 630-214-0564

ORDERING INFORMATION
web: *www.bookjungle.com*
email: *sales@bookjungle.com*
fax: *630-214-0564*
mail: *Book Jungle PO Box 2226 Champaign, IL 61825*
or PayPal *to sales@bookjungle.com*

Please contact us for bulk discounts

DIRECT-ORDER TERMS

20% Discount if You Order Two or More Books
Free Domestic Shipping!
Accepted: Master Card, Visa, Discover, American Express

www.ingramcontent.com/pod-product-compliance
Lightning Source LLC
Chambersburg PA
CBHW080508110426
42742CB00017B/3038